PREFACE

1. Scope

This publication is the keystone document for the communications system series of publications. It provides the doctrinal foundation for communications system support of joint operations across the range of military operations.

2. Purpose

This publication has been prepared under the direction of the Chairman of the Joint Chiefs of Staff (CJCS). It sets forth joint doctrine to govern the activities and performance of the Armed Forces of the United States in operations and provides the doctrinal basis for interagency coordination and for US military involvement in multinational operations. It provides military guidance for the exercise of authority by combatant commanders and other joint force commanders (JFCs) and prescribes joint doctrine for operations and training. It provides military guidance for use by the Armed Forces in preparing their appropriate plans. It is not the intent of this publication to restrict the authority of the JFC from organizing the force and executing the mission in a manner the JFC deems most appropriate to ensure unity of effort in the accomplishment of the overall objective.

3. Application

a. Joint doctrine established in this publication applies to the commanders of combatant commands, subunified commands, joint task forces, subordinate components of these commands, and the Services.

b. The guidance in this publication is authoritative; as such, this doctrine will be followed except when, in the judgment of the commander, exceptional circumstances dictate otherwise. If conflicts arise between the contents of this publication and the contents of Service publications, this publication will take precedence unless the CJCS, normally in coordination with the other members of the Joint Chiefs of Staff, has provided more current and specific guidance. Commanders of forces operating as part of a multinational (alliance or coalition) military command should follow multinational doctrine and procedures ratified by the United States. For doctrine and procedures not ratified by the United States, commanders should evaluate and follow the multinational command's doctrine and procedures, where applicable and consistent with US law, regulations, and doctrine.

Intentionally Blank

- **Updates the role of United States Strategic Command in operating and defending the Global Information Grid (GIG)**

- **Updates information on Cyberspace and the role of United States Cyber Command**

- **Updates Network Operations**

- **Updates the GIG characteristics**

- **Discusses the "Aerial Layer"**

- **Corrects factual errors due to procedural and organizational changes**

Intentionally Blank

TABLE OF CONTENTS

CHAPTER V

COMMUNICATIONS SYSTEM SUPPORT TO THE PRESIDENT, THE SECRETARY OF DEFENSE, AND THE INTELLIGENCE COMMUNITY

APPENDIX

GLOSSARY

FIGURE

Intentionally Blank

- **Provides an Overview of Joint Communications System Objectives, Roles, Functions, and Principles**

- **Describes the Global Information Grid**

- **Discusses Joint Force Communications System Operations Planning and Management**

- **Describes Joint Force Network Operations**

- **Describes Communications System Support to the President, Secretary of Defense, the Joint Chiefs of Staff, and the Intelligence Community**

Overview

Effective command and control (C2) is necessary for proper integration and employment of operational capabilities.

The objective of the joint communications system is to assist the joint force commander (JFC) in command and control (C2) of military operations. While C2 alone will neither destroy an adversary target nor accomplish emergency resupply, no single activity in military operations is more important.

The first element of C2 system is **people** — people who acquire information, make decisions, take action, communicate, and collaborate with one another to accomplish a common goal. The second element of the C2 system taken collectively are the **facilities, equipment, communications, and procedures** essential to a commander for planning, directing, and controlling operations of assigned forces pursuant to the missions assigned. Although families of hardware are often referred to as "systems," the C2 system is more than simply equipment. High-quality equipment and advanced technology do not guarantee effective C2. Effective C2 starts with well-trained and qualified people and an effective guiding philosophy and procedures.

The communications system has multiple roles.

One role of the communications system is to ensure connectivity throughout the operational area, thus providing JFCs with the capability to effectively plan, conduct, and sustain joint operations. A second role is to provide JFCs the principal tool with which they collect, transport, process, protect, and disseminate information. Through the exchange of information, effective C2 integrates joint force components, allowing them to function effectively across vast distances in austere or complex environments and in all weather conditions. The third role of the communications system is to provide processes and procedures which help ensure information availability to facilitate joint and multinational operations.

Communications system functions.

The communications system supporting US military forces must have the capability to rapidly adapt to changing demands; to provide information that is **needed** (the right information); **where needed** (the right place); and **when needed** (the right time), protected from interception and exploitation and presented in an actionable format. By meeting these fundamental objectives, the communications system allows joint forces to seize opportunity and meet mission objectives.

A joint force linked and synchronized in time and purpose is considered **networked**. The joint force capitalizes on information and near simultaneous dissemination to turn information into actions. An effective communications system helps the JFC conduct distributed operations in a nonlinear battlespace. To do this, the communications system must be **interoperable, agile, trusted, and shared.**

Global Information Grid

The Global Information Grid is the globally interconnected end-to-end set of information capabilities, associated processes and personnel for collecting, processing, storing, dissemination and managing information on demand to joint forces and support personnel.

The Global Information Grid (GIG) is the Department of Defense's (DOD's) globally interconnected, end-to-end set of information capabilities, associated processes, and personnel for collecting, processing, storing, disseminating, and managing information on demand to joint forces and support personnel. The GIG includes all owned and leased communications and computing systems and services, software (including applications), data, security services, and other associated services necessary to achieve information security. It also includes national security systems as defined in section 5142 of the Clinger-Cohen Act of 1996. The GIG supports all DOD, national security, related intelligence community missions and functions (strategic, operational, tactical, and business), in war and in peace. The GIG provides capabilities from all operating locations (bases, posts, camps, stations, facilities, mobile platforms and deployed sites). The GIG provides interfaces to multinational and non-DOD users and systems. Therefore, from a service-oriented perspective, the GIG can be viewed as a set of computing platforms, weapons systems, and sensors exchanging information through a globally interconnected network. DOD's strategy is to empower the joint force with the information needed to achieve successful military operations by integrating the seven components of the GIG described in this publication.

GIG components are categorized as **warrior, global applications, computing, communications, foundation, information management, and network operations (NETOPS).**

Defense Information Systems Network (DISN). The DISN is the major element of the GIG. It has three segments: sustaining base, long haul, and deployed. It is DOD's worldwide enterprise-level telecommunications infrastructure providing end-to-end information transfer for supporting military operations. For the most part, it is transparent to the joint force. The DISN facilitates the management of information resources, and is responsive to national security, as well as DOD needs. It provides GIG network services to DOD installations and deployed forces. Those services include voice, data, and video, as well as enterprise services such as directories and messaging. DOD policy mandates the use of the DISN for wide area and metropolitan networks.

Commander United States Strategic Command (CDRUSSTRATCOM) has overall responsibility for global network operations and defense in coordination with the Chairman of the Joint Chiefs of Staff (CJCS) and the other combatant commands. United States Cyber Command (USCYBERCOM), a subordinate unified command under United States Strategic Command (USSTRATCOM), focuses on military cyberspace operations. Combatant commanders (CCDRs) coordinate with USSTRATCOM through USCYBERCOM to ensure global impacts to the GIG are properly considered. The duties previously assigned to Joint Task Force-Global Network Operations (JTF-GNO) under Defense Information Systems Agency and Joint Functional Component Command for Network Warfare under USSTRATCOM are the responsibility of USCYBERCOM. Because the GIG represents the entire communications system of Department of Defense, there remain many decisions regarding planning and design that fall under the purview of the Assistant Secretary of Defense (Networks and Information Integration (ASD[NII]), who is also designated DOD's chief information officer (CIO). Many of those decisions involve the insertion of new technology as well as other architectural standards, which may impact the interoperability of the DOD as a whole.

The GIG operates, through cyberspace, as a globally interconnected, end-to-end, interoperable network-of-networks, that combines the communications system capabilities of the DOD components and spans traditional boundaries of authority. Operation and defense of the GIG is largely a matter of overarching common processes, standards, and protocols orchestrated by USSTRATCOM.

ASD(NII), as the DOD CIO, serves as DOD's principal staff assistant for information management (IM), and consequently develops and issues the DOD IM strategic plan. **The DOD CIO is the GIG architect and is overall responsible for developing, maintaining, and enforcing compliance with the GIG architecture.**

Unless otherwise directed, communications between the President and the Secretary of Defense (SecDef) and the combatant commanders (CCDRs) are transmitted through CJCS. **CJCS** exercises operational oversight over those portions of the GIG utilized for such communications. CJCS is responsible for the operation of the National Military Command System (NMCS) for SecDef to meet the needs of the President, SecDef, and the Joint Chiefs of Staff (JCS); and establishes operational policies and procedures for all components of the NMCS and ensures their implementation. The Director Command, Control, Communications, and Computer Systems, (Joint Staff J-6) and joint community warfighter CIO provides advice and recommendations about communications system matters to the CJCS.

The **Military Communications-Electronics Board** (MCEB) is a decision-making instrument of CJCS and SecDef for determining corporate communications system strategy to support the joint force. The MCEB is chaired by the Joint Staff J-6 and composed of over twenty organizations from the Services and DOD agencies at the flag officer/Senior Executive Service level.

The **Combined Communications-Electronics Board** (CCEB) is a five-nation joint military communications organization whose mission is the coordination of any military communications system matter that is referred to it by a member nation. The US representative for the CCEB is the Joint Staff J-6, who also chairs the MCEB.

Combatant commanders oversee and coordinate GIG planning and employment within their areas of responsibility. They utilize the JTF-GNO, the theater network operations center (TNC) hierarchy, as well as Service component command TNCs as appropriate, and joint control centers. To this end, they collaborate with their respective Service components, Defense Information Systems Agency, Defense Intelligence Agency (DIA), and USSTRATCOM to create and maintain visibility over theater networks.

Military Departments and Services provide an interoperable and compatible communications system for the effective prosecution of military operations and plan for the expansion of the GIG to meet the requirements of DOD.

The **JFC,** through the communications system directorate of a joint staff (J-6), ensures an adequate and effective communications system is available to support the joint force C2 infrastructure via system plans, annexes, and operating instructions to support the assigned mission and by providing overall management of the communications system supporting the JFC. As the forces deploy, the joint force J-6 establishes a joint network operations control center to establish network control and management within the operational area.

DOD agencies, such as DIA, National Security Agency, and National Geospatial-Intelligence Agency, are responsible for ensuring that their information systems environment is developed and maintained in a manner that is consistent with and reflective of the GIG architecture, and that agency-specific programs are planned, resourced, acquired, and implemented in accordance with the DOD Information Management Support Plan and DOD resource priorities.

Essential elements of the communications system are driven by the mission and determined by the C2 organization and location of forces assigned to the joint force commander.

Communications system planners are responsible for ensuring that the organization's communications network can facilitate a rapid, unconstrained flow of information from its source through intermediate collection and processing nodes to its delivery to the user. Communications system planners should clearly understand the capabilities and limitations of all potentially available strategic, operational, and tactical communications systems and equipment, whether they are organic to Services and agencies, belong to non-US forces, are commercial, or provided by a host nation. Building the communications system to support the JFC requires knowledge of the joint force organization, the commander's concept of operations, communications available, and how they are employed. The J-6 is responsible for planning and establishing the communications system and the communications estimate of supportability during course of action development and selection under the crisis action planning process.

Planning considerations.

There are several key considerations in communications system planning. Important is the establishment of computer network defense to achieve information assurance. The integration of multinational communications system operations, often composed of multinational partners with diverse groups of security and information sharing domains must be planned and managed. Planners must consider that the communications system is the primary means through which intelligence, surveillance, and reconnaissance information flows to the joint force and, therefore, planning must be conducted in close coordination with the intelligence directorate of a joint staff. Of increasing importance to joint operations is effective connectivity to non-DOD departments and agencies and nongovernmental and intergovernmental organizations. Additionally, communications system planners and managers must consider the complexities of world wide web and public internet access, information dissemination management, and joint network communications control. Satellite communications planning is a critical item. As is integration of the aerial layer with the space and terrestrial layers. Finally, communications planners and managers must optimize the use (access) of electromagnetic spectrum for all electromagnetic spectrum dependent systems through sound planning and adherence to frequency assignment doctrine.

Communications planning focuses on five areas of analysis:

Mission Analysis

Information needs

Interoperability, compatibility, and supportability

Capability

Communications planning is divided into five areas: mission analysis, information needs analysis, interoperability and compatibility analysis, capability analysis, and allocation of communications system assets. During **mission analysis**, communications system planners develop the communications system estimate and specified and implied tasks to be performed by operators and communications system personnel. **Information needs are analyzed** by working closely with all functional communities to develop information exchange requirements, which identify products to be transmitted and received, as well as the throughput, quantity, and characteristics of those products. Planners also identify **interoperability, compatibility, and supportability** requirements and assess them against documented capabilities, assessing any shortfalls or deficiencies for operational and mission impact. Based on these first three areas, planners conduct a **capability analysis** to identify the communications equipment and networks that have the capability to support the operation plan. This analysis is a daily assessment during all phases of the operation. Finally, after the template is developed, joint force and component planners must examine all available

Allocation of communications system assets.

resources and **allocate communications system assets** to form a tailored communications system.

Among the many important planning factors associated with the communications system, three stand out. First, the communications system director and staff must be involved in the planning process early and must understand the concept of operations to provide communications advice to the JFC during the planning process. Secondly, the plan, as it is being developed, must be constantly assessed for feasibility and adequacy to satisfy the joint force's information requirements. Finally, although communications system planning takes place in coordination with the other planning elements of a joint staff, communications system planners must anticipate user requirements throughout all phases of joint operations. Therefore, plans and initial communications system support must be incrementally developed, deployed, and employed to meet the JFC's continually evolving mission.

Effective network operations culminates in assured service to the joint force facilitating network enabled operations.

NETOPS provides integrated network visibility and end-to-end management of networks, global applications, and services across the GIG. Network visibility enables commanders to manage their networks as they would other combat systems. **The NETOPS mission is to operate and defend the GIG.** Unlike many missions that are deemed successful at a defined completion date, the NETOPS mission is perpetual, requiring continual support to be successful. **The effectiveness of NETOPS** is measured in terms of availability and reliability of network enabled services, across all areas of interest, in adherence to agreed-upon service levels and policies. **The purpose of NETOPS** is assured system and network availability, assured information protection, and assured information delivery, which protect and maintain freedom of action for DOD missions within cyberspace.

As the DOD CIO, the Office of the ASD(NII) is responsible for the policy and architecture for NETOPS. CJCS maintains operational oversight of the GIG through the National Military Command Center and USSTRATCOM. USSTRATCOM has the Unified Command Plan mission to operate and defend the GIG. CDRUSSTRATCOM has delegated operational and tactical level planning and day-today management of the operations and defense of the GIG to USCYBERCOM.

President, Secretary of Defense, Joint Chiefs of Staff, and Intelligence Community Support

The National Military Command System communicates warning and intelligence to commanders.

The NMCS is the priority component of the GIG designed to support the President, SecDef, and the JCS in the exercise of their responsibilities. The NMCS provides the means by which the President and SecDef can receive warning and intelligence so decisions can be made, the resources of the military Services can be applied, military missions can be assigned, and direction can be communicated to CCDRs or the commanders of other commands.

The joint intelligence systems architecture is an integral part of the GIG, and consists of an integrated network supporting voice, data, and video-teleconferencing. The Joint Worldwide Intelligence Communications System, the joint deployable intelligence support system, and the distributed common ground system currently form the foundation of the sensitive compartmented information portion of the GIG.

The National Communications System (NCS), consisting of federal member departments and agencies, is responsible for ensuring the availability of a viable national security and emergency preparedness telecommunications infrastructure. The NCS consists of the telecommunications assets of the entities represented on the NCS Committee of Principals and an administrative structure consisting of the executive agent, the NCS Committee of Principals, and the manager.

CONCLUSION

This keystone publication identifies approved doctrine for communications system support to joint operations and outlines the responsibilities of Services, agencies, and combatant commands with respect to ensuring effective communications support to commanders. It addresses how communications system support the conduct of joint operations, including how systems are to be configured, deployed, and employed. Finally, this publication provides guidance necessary to plan, manage, employ, execute and train for communications system support at the operational and tactical level of joint operations.

CHAPTER I
INTRODUCTION

> *"Fighting with a large army under your command is nowise different from fighting with a small one: it is merely a question of instituting signs and signals."*
>
> **Sun Tzu**
> **The Art of War**

1. Introduction

The objective of the joint communications system is to assist the joint force commander (JFC) in command and control (C2) of military operations. Effective C2 is vital for proper integration and employment of operational capabilities. The Department of Defense's (DOD's) end-to-end communications system supporting the JFC is the Global Information Grid (GIG). The GIG includes all joint and Service communications as well as interfaces to non-DOD and multinational users (see Chapter II, "The Global Information Grid"). The GIG unifies DOD's networks into a single real-time information system to provide increased information capabilities to the joint force. It should be understood that communications systems are more than electronic boxes, wires, and radio signals and the GIG is more than a computer network. The interdependence of the parts, as well as the processes, policy, and data on those systems, permeate daily life, and preparation for and execution of operations.

2. Command and Control

a. No single activity in military operations is more important than C2. Alone, C2 will not destroy a single adversary target or affect a single emergency resupply. Yet, none of these essential joint force activities, or any others, would be possible without effective C2. A superior communications system helps commanders to maintain the unity of effort to apply their forces' capabilities at the critical times and places to win.

b. Often, C2 is thought of as a distinct and specialized function — like logistics, intelligence, electronic warfare, or administration — with its own peculiar methods, considerations, and vocabulary, and occurring independently of other functions. In fact, **C2 encompasses all military functions and operations, synchronizing them into a meaningful whole.** C2 is the means by which a commander recognizes what needs to be done and sees to it that appropriate actions are taken.

c. **Elements of the Command and Control System**

(1) The first element of a C2 system is **people** — people who acquire information, make decisions, take action, communicate, and collaborate with one another to accomplish a common goal. Human beings — from the senior commander framing a strategic concept to a junior Service member calling in a situation report — are integral components of the C2 system and not merely users.

(2) The second element of the C2 system taken collectively are the **facilities, equipment, communications, and procedures** essential to a commander for planning, directing, and controlling operations of assigned forces pursuant to the missions assigned. Although families of hardware are often referred to as "systems," the C2 system is more than simply equipment. High-quality equipment and advanced technology do not guarantee effective C2. Effective C2 starts with well-trained and qualified people and an effective guiding philosophy and procedures.

d. **Quality of Information.** In one way or another, C2 is essentially about information: getting it, judging its value, processing it into useful form, acting on it, and sharing it with others. **There are two basic uses for information. The first is to help create situational awareness (SA) as the basis for a decision. The second is to direct and coordinate actions in the execution of the decision.** The communications system must present information in a form that is both quickly understood and useful to the recipient. Many sources of information are imperfect and susceptible to distortion and deception. The seven criteria shown in Figure I-1 help characterize information quality. Combining pieces of information with context produces ideas or provides knowledge. C2 is as much a problem of information management (IM) as it is of carrying out other warfighting tasks. **Good IM makes accomplishment of other tasks less complex.** Automation and standardization of communications system processes and procedures improve IM and assist the commander's effectiveness and speed of C2. Today, improved technology in mobility, weapons, sensors, and communications continues to reduce reaction time, increase the tempo of operations, and generate large amounts of information. If information is not well managed the reactions of commanders and decisionmakers and ultimately the joint force may be degraded. It is essential that the communications system complement human capabilities and reduce or eliminate known limitations.

e. **A well crafted and coordinated set of integrated, interoperable procedures is important** to operating in a joint, multinational, and interagency context of current and future operations. The value of technology, organization, and strategy is diminished in the absence of a professional force to leverage their value. To meet uncertain challenges on the horizon, communications system professionals must be fully indoctrinated in employment of joint and multinational warfighting capabilities. They must also be trained to anticipate and counter the dynamics of an asymmetric adversary. A comprehensive and thoroughly rehearsed set of operational procedures is crucial to developing that required degree of proficiency. The communications system must be of sufficient scale, capacity, reach, and reliability to support evolving operational and training missions. Additionally, the communications system must integrate new technologies into a robust, standards-based, network enabled environment, to facilitate delivery of the right information to the right location at the right time in an actionable format.

INFORMATION QUALITY CRITERIA

ACCURACY

- Information that conveys the true situation

RELEVANCE

- Information that applies to the mission, task, or situation ahead

TIMELINESS

- Information that is available in time to make decisions

USABILITY

- Information that is understandable and is in commonly understood format and displays

COMPLETENESS

- All necessary information required by the decisionmaker

BREVITY

- Information that has only the level of detail required

SECURITY

- Information that has been afforded adequate protection where required

Figure I-1. Information Quality Criteria

3. The Role of the Communications System

a. A secure and robust communications system gives the JFC the means to assimilate information and to exercise authority and direct forces over large geographic areas and a wide range of conditions. A communications system that provides connectivity throughout the battlespace is vital to planning, conducting, and sustaining operations. Tactical operations routinely require long-range, mobile communications.

The JFC must maintain reliable and secure communications with superior and subordinate commanders during all phases of an operation. The communications system must be of sufficient scale, accessibility, capacity, reach, and reliability to support evolving operational and training missions. Consideration must be made for en route, intratheater, and intertheater communications. In addition, the communications system must be prepared to interface with governmental and nongovernmental organizations (NGOs), local officials, and multinational forces.

b. The communications system is the JFC's principal tool to collect, transport, process, protect, and disseminate information. Given the criticality of information, the security of the communications system is paramount to ensuring the JFC can trust the information it provides. Effective C2, through the exchange of information, integrates joint force components, allowing them to function effectively across vast distances in austere or complex environments and in all weather conditions. The mission and structure of the joint force drives specific information flow and processing requirements. The location and information requirements of the joint force drive the specific configuration of the JFC's communications system. The goal is to provide rapid information sharing to facilitate a common understanding of the current situation — a common operational picture (COP).

c. Processes and procedures help ensure information availability and access across the operational environment, and facilitate:

(1) **Joint and Multinational Operations and Interagency Coordination.** The communications system facilitates joint and multinational operations and interagency coordination by providing the means to share operational area visualization; manage information; and facilitate collaborative planning, rehearsal, execution, and assessment with joint and multinational forces and other government agencics (OGAs).

(2) **Strategic Agility.** The communications system supports the rapid deployment and employment of task-organized forces anywhere in the world. Rapid information sharing around the globe permits simultaneous, interactive planning from widely dispersed locations, thereby allowing the use of remote staffs to develop and coordinate an operation plan (OPLAN), and execute an operation order (OPORD). It provides JFCs the ability to reach back to data repositories, thereby increasing deployability, reducing footprint, and enhancing access to global intelligence, surveillance, and reconnaissance (ISR) assets. The communications system supports a collaborative information environment that assists JFCs in conducting detailed, concurrent, and parallel planning.

(3) **Operational Reach.** The communications system supports the synchronization of warfighting functions, allowing commanders to locate and identify friendly forces in the battlespace and support the conduct of over-the-horizon operations with beyond line-of-sight communications and communications on the move.

(4) **Tactical Flexibility.** The communications system allows the joint force to enhance SA and timely decisionmaking; rapidly and positively identify and engage targets; and develop and conduct operations across the range of military operations. The communications system supports the development and employment of the commander's intent and planning guidance to foster decentralized execution. Timely delivery of information concerning targets, movement of forces, condition of equipment, levels of supplies, and disposition of assets — both friendly and adversary — to the joint force allows decentralized execution.

(5) **Network Enabled Operations**

(a) The modern communications system allows the interconnection (networking) of geographically separated forces which permits network enabled operations. Network enabled operations are military operations that exploit state-of-the-art information and networking technology to integrate widely dispersed human decisionmakers, situational and targeting sensors, and forces and weapons into a highly adaptive, comprehensive system. Network enabled operations exploits the combat power derived from the robust networking of well informed, geographically dispersed forces. A networked force can increase combat power, achieving greater speed of command decisions and increasing the lethality, survivability, and responsiveness of the force.

(b) At times, improvements in technology result in leaps in capability. The networking of the joint force has brought about such a leap. The communications system enables collaborative planning, the COP, control of manned and unmanned tactical reconnaissance and attack platforms, increased visibility of logistic assets, and a reduced footprint through remote staffing.

(6) **Information Superiority (IS)**

(a) The communications system facilitates IS. Information and IM lie at the core of every military activity. Throughout history, military leaders have recognized that a competitive advantage in this aspect of military operations is a key contributor to victory in battle. This advantage, or imbalance, in one's favor within the information environment is called IS. However, IS is more than having an edge over an adversary. It is more than just sustaining the information needs of our own forces. It also involves denying an adversary's ability to do the same (see Figure I-2).

(b) The power of superiority in the information environment mandates that the United States fights for it as a first priority even before hostilities begin. This requires DOD to develop doctrine, tactics, techniques, and procedures (TTP), organizational relationships, and technologies to win this fight. The quality of information depends upon the accuracy, timeliness, relevance, usability, and completeness of information from all sources. A priority responsibility of command is to ensure access to all relevant information sources within and among all DOD and non-DOD organizations, and in multinational operations with mission partners. The **continuous sharing of information** from a variety of sources facilitates enabling the

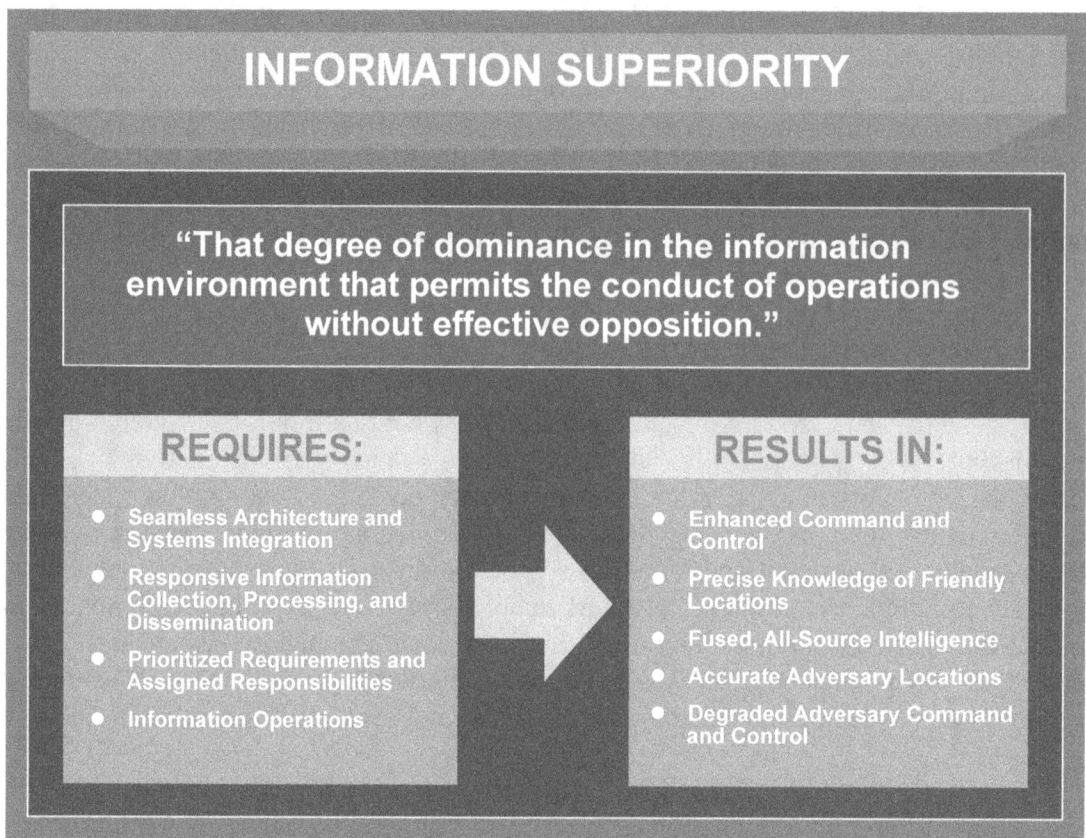

Figure I-2. Information Superiority

fully networked joint force to achieve shared SA among DOD components, all levels of US Government, multinational partners, and the private sector.

(7) Cyberspace

(a) Cyberspace is a global domain within the information environment consisting of the interdependent network of information technology (IT) infrastructures, including the Internet, telecommunications networks, computer systems, and embedded processors and controllers. Cyberspace threats are a real and imminent danger to GIG operations and information. Information is crucial to the success of joint and multinational operations. Information is also a critical instrument of national power, and the ability to achieve and maintain an advantage in cyberspace is crucial to national security. The GIG through cyberspace provides the valuable service of assured information transport, storage, and delivery for the owners and authorized users of the information. Networks and network operations (NETOPS) are the means by which DOD manages the flow of information over the GIG. Because all DOD components need the ability to operate unhindered in cyberspace, this presents a unique challenge. We are not the sole users or occupants of cyberspace nor is our participation isolated or without the presence of sophisticated adversaries who challenge us daily. Our joint forces, mission partners, and first responders demand communications that are not only secure, but also flexible enough to meet the ever-changing requirements demanded by joint and multinational operations.

4. Communications System Functions

a. The communications system supporting US military forces must have the capability to rapidly adapt to changing demands and to provide information that is **needed** (the right information), **where needed** (the right place), and **when needed** (the right time), protected from interception and exploitation and presented in a useful format. By meeting these fundamental objectives, the communications system allows joint forces to seize on opportunity and meet mission objectives. The communications system facilitates information sharing and decision support and is an essential building block in today's operational environment.

b. Information systems that make up the communications system normally have the capabilities of acquisition, processing, storage, transport, control, protection, dissemination, and presentation (see Figure I-3).

(1) **Acquisition** is the introduction of information into the communications system. Information sources include feeds from manned or autonomous sensors, radar data streams, video capture, manual input, or any other source that inserts information into the communications system.

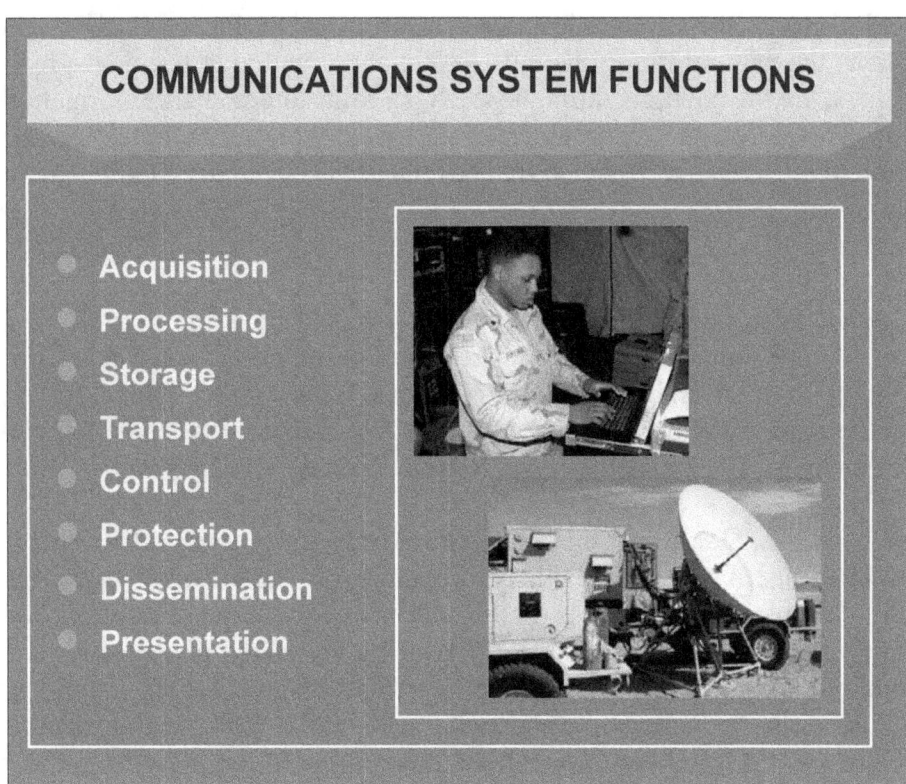

Figure I-3. Communications System Functions

(2) **Processing** is a specified sequence of operations performed on well-defined inputs to produce a specified output. This activity is typically used for manipulating data, information, and/or knowledge into the desired form to support decisionmakers.

(3) The **storage** capability is the retention, organization, and disposition of data, information, and/or knowledge to facilitate information sharing and retrieval.

(4) The communications system normally requires a **transport** capability to support end-to-end information exchange and dissemination in a global environment.

(5) The purpose of the **control** component is to direct, monitor, and regulate other communications system functions toward the fulfillment of joint force requirements within specified performance parameters. Control activities are more commonly referred to as NETOPS, and can be policy or technically oriented. The NETOPS function and the subcomponents are further discussed in Chapter II, "The Global Information Grid," and Chapter IV, "Network Operations."

(6) **Protection.** Ensuring information integrity, secure processing, and transmission with access only by authorized personnel.

(7) **Dissemination.** Distributing processed information to the appropriate users of the information.

(8) Finally, the communications system must interface with the users. This is referred to as the **presentation** function. Telephones, computer terminals, radar screens, among others, are the conduits through which the joint forces share information with one another. Therefore, the communications system must facilitate presentation of information to the user in the method that best facilitates its understanding and use.

5. Communications System Principles

a. A joint force that is linked and synchronized in time and purpose is considered networked. The joint force capitalizes on information and near simultaneous dissemination to turn information into actions. Networked joint forces increase operational effectiveness by allowing dispersed forces to more efficiently communicate, maneuver, share a COP, and achieve the desired end state.

b. A networked force has the ability to expand its operational reach by allowing dispersed elements to use nonorganic information services of other organizations. By integrating information from across the breadth of the battlespace, the joint force is able to maintain more relevant and complete SA. This integrated picture allows the JFC to better employ the right capabilities, in the right place, and at the right time. In order to achieve this capability, unity of command is essential. An effective communications system helps the JFC conduct distributed operations in a nonlinear battlespace. To do this, the communications system must be **interoperable, agile, trusted, and shared** (see Figure I-4).

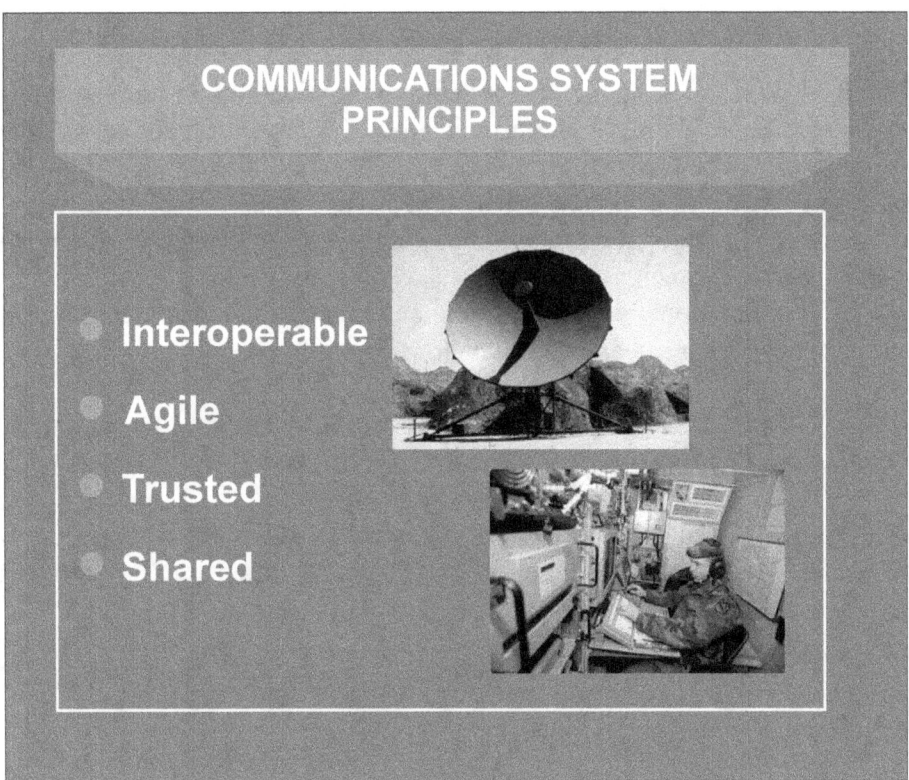

Figure I-4. Communications System Principles

(1) **Interoperability** is the ability of two or more systems or components to exchange information and to use the information that has been exchanged. Interoperability is key to the joint force gaining IS in today's network enabled environment. Interoperability facilitates rapid availability of the communications system and enables collaboration among joint forces, with OGAs, NGOs, and other mission partners. Common policies and standards and to some extent procedures is the preferred method of achieving interoperability. Although DOD does not control multinational communications standards, the Combined Communications-Electronics Board (CCEB) is a multinational organization that focuses entirely on command, control communications systems interoperability. Other methods to achieve some degree of interoperability include: commonality, compatibility of equipment, and liaison.

(a) Equipment and systems are **common** when they can be operated and maintained by personnel trained on any one of the systems without additional specialized training and their repair parts and consumable items (components or subassemblies) are interchangeable.

(b) **Compatibility of equipment** is the capability of two or more items or components of equipment or material to exist or function in the same system or environment without mutual interference. All forms of compatibility, including electromagnetic compatibility and frequency supportability, must be considered at the earliest conceptual stages and throughout the planning, design, development, testing and evaluation, and operational life cycle of all systems.

(c) **Standardization.** The broad objectives of the National Communications System (NCS), the GIG, and the Defense Information Systems Network (DISN), coupled with the need for the tactical communications system to interface with facilities of the DISN, require the communications system interfaces be standardized as much as practical. The objectives of interface standardization are to minimize the requirement for ad hoc field patches to compensate for noncompliance with interface standards; achieve the maximum economy possible from cross-servicing and cross-procurement; permit emergency supply assistance among Services; facilitate interoperability of functionally similar joint and Service communications; and avoid unnecessary duplication in research and development of new technology.

(d) **Liaison.** Lastly, gaining interoperability among joint and multinational forces as well as interactions with OGAs and NGOs can be aided by liaison.

(2) **Agile.** To support agile forces and operational concepts, the communications system must also be agile. The key dimensions of communications system agility are:

(a) **Responsiveness** — the ability to react to a change in the environment in a timely manner.

(b) **Flexibility** — the ability to employ multiple ways to succeed and the capacity to move seamlessly between them.

(c) **Innovation** — the ability to do new things and the ability to do old things in new ways.

(d) **Adaptation** — the ability to change work processes and the ability to change the organization.

(3) **Trusted.** The joint force must have confidence in the capabilities of the network and the validity of the information made available by the network.

(a) **Survivable.** The security of information and the communications system also involves procedural and technical aspects, integral to the defensive operation. These include:

1. **Physical security** of the communications system components and facilities.

2. **Personnel security** of individuals authorized access to the communications system.

3. **Operations security** (OPSEC) procedures and techniques protecting operational employment of the communications system components.

<u>4.</u> **Denying** the adversary information about specific communications system configuration, operational employment, and degree of component importance to mission accomplishment.

<u>5.</u> **Low probability of intercept** (LPI) and **low probability of detection** (LPD) capabilities and techniques designed to defeat adversary attempts to detect and exploit the communications system transmission media.

<u>6.</u> **Emissions control** procedures designed to support OPSEC and LPI/LPD objectives.

<u>7.</u> **Communications system design and configuration control** to manage security through control of communications system component design and manufacturing, and control of changes made to hardware, software, firmware, documentation, and testing throughout the life cycle of the communications system.

<u>8.</u> Identifying technological and procedural **vulnerability analysis and assessment** programs.

<u>9.</u> **Robustness** — the ability to maintain effectiveness across a range of tasks, situations, and conditions.

<u>10.</u> **Resilience** — the ability to rapidly recover from or adjust to misfortune, damage, or a destabilizing event in the environment.

(b) **Protected.** The JFC conducts defensive operations to protect assigned and attached forces, including communications system assets. Since the communications system and associated forces are crucial enablers for joint C2, they present a high-value target to the adversary and must be protected to maintain the integrity of the joint force C2 system. Information assurance (IA) is employed to ensure the security of information and the communications system through information protection, intrusion/attack detection and effect isolation, and incident response to restore information and system security. The IA construct consists of maintaining network availability, protecting data integrity, enforcing confidentiality, authentication and nonrepudiation, or verifiability of the trust source. IA measures are taken to protect and defend network and information availability and data integrity objectives. IA is discussed more thoroughly in Chapter IV, "Network Operations."

<u>1.</u> **Computer Network Defense (CND).** Actions taken to protect, monitor, analyze, detect, and respond to unauthorized activity within DOD information systems and computer networks. CND also employs intelligence, counterintelligence, law enforcement, and other military capabilities to defend DOD information and computer networks. CND employs IA capabilities to respond to unauthorized activity within DOD information systems and computer networks in response to a CND alert or threat information. DOD's CND mission is global and focuses on protection and defense

of DOD's interconnected systems and networks. To protect the communications system, CND measures are employed with a defense-in-depth strategy.

2. **Communications Security (COMSEC).** COMSEC capabilities are used to protect information transiting terminal devices and transmission media from adversary exploitation to include transmission security capabilities designed to support OPSEC and LPI/LPD.

(c) **Sustainable.** The communications system must provide continuous support during any type and length of operation. This requires economical design and employment of the communications system without sacrificing operational capability or survivability. The following are some examples that may be used to improve system sustainability:

1. Consolidation of functionally similar facilities which are closely located under one command or Service.

2. Careful planning, design, and procurement of facilities and systems.

3. Efficient management and operating practices and effective communications system discipline.

4. Maximum use of the DISN common-user subsystems.

5. Judicious use of commercial services.

6. Adherence to approved architectures.

(4) **Shared.** Information sharing allows for the mutual use of information services or capabilities. This ability may cross functional or organizational boundaries. Information sharing is facilitated by global authentication, access control, and directory services which allows any authorized user, with common and portable identity credentials, to have access to, and visibility of, all appropriate operational, business support, or intelligence related information, services, and applications related to their mission and communities of interest (COIs).

6. **Joint Communications System Roles and Responsibilities**

a. Combatant commanders (CCDRs) should be familiar with the guidance in DOD Instruction (DODI) 8410.02, NETOPS for the GIG.

b. The Director Command, Control, Communications, and Computer Systems, **(Joint Staff J-6)** provides advice and recommendations about communications system matters to the Chairman of the Joint Chiefs of Staff (CJCS). In accordance with (IAW) Chairman of the Joint Chiefs of Staff Instruction (CJCSI) 8010.01A, *Joint Community Chief Information Officer*, the Joint Staff J-6 also serves as the joint community chief information officer (CIO). As chairman of the Military Communications-Electronics

Board (MCEB), the Director, J-6 utilizes the MCEB to coordinate and resolve GIG issues among the Services and member agencies. With respect to joint force support, under CJCS authority and direction, and subject to the supervision and guidance of the Director, Joint Staff (DJS), the Director, J-6 normally has the responsibility to:

(1) Allocate CJCS-controlled communications system assets for use during real-world operations and assist non-DOD users in gaining access to military satellite communications (SATCOM) resources.

(2) Advise the DJS and the Operations Directorate of the Joint Staff (J-3) on combatant commands' communications system readiness to execute assigned missions and, in cases of deficiencies, recommend and facilitate corrective action.

(3) Evaluate operational feasibility and adequacy of communications system support for current joint war plans as well as emergency, contingency, and OPLANs submitted by DOD agencies, combatant commands, and international treaty organizations, and initiate required corrective action.

(4) In coordination with United States Joint Forces Command (USJFCOM) and United States Strategic Command (USSTRATCOM), evaluate the effectiveness of the communications system of the National Military Command System (NMCS) and combatant commands. In collaboration with J-3 and Director for Operational Plans and Joint Force Development, direct or recommend new procedures, programs, or systems to achieve improved capabilities.

(5) Provide the communications system staff augmentation support for crisis, contingency, or emergencies in support of J-3.

(6) Review communications system requirements submitted by the CCDRs and ensure adequacy and consistency with operational and logistic near- and long-term plans in coordination with J-3, logistics directorate of a joint staff (J-4), and Joint Staff Plans Directorate.

(7) In coordination with the J-3, and the Assistant Secretary of Defense for Networks and Information Integration (ASD[NII]), ensure that life cycle management of joint C2 systems has the capability to support the President, the Office of the Secretary of Defense (OSD), Joint Staff, Services, combatant commands, DOD agencies, and any other entity that may comprise a joint operation.

(8) In coordination with J-3, J-4, and the ASD(NII)/DOD CIO, provide technical and programmatic oversight of the Global Command and Control System (GCCS) family of systems and the Global Combat Support System-Joint (GCSS-J) to ensure effective communications system operation for users.

(9) Make recommendations about protection of the joint and multinational communications system from adversary activities.

(10) Act as the primary Joint Staff point of contact to provide centralized direction and management for the nuclear communications system.

(11) Recommend US military positions for North Atlantic Treaty Organization (NATO) command, control, and communications matters (including long-term DOD program; rationalization, standardization, and interoperability matters; and C2 architecture) that affect areas of the communications system.

(12) In coordination with the J-3, advocate the implementation of collaborative information capabilities and supporting environments to enable information sharing.

(13) In coordination with the CCDRs, identify NETOPS capabilities needed to support joint, multinational, and other operations with mission partners.

c. The communications system directorate of a joint staff (J-6) at the combatant command level is generally responsible to:

(1) Ensure that communications system personnel, COMSEC, and equipment requirements of the JFC are supported.

(2) Coordinate communications system activities with CJCS, USSTRATCOM, United States Cyber Command (USCYBERCOM), Defense Information Systems Agency (DISA), Services, combatant commands, component forces, and others, as appropriate.

(3) Prepare communications system policy and guidance to enable subordinate forces to operate within the unified command structure.

(4) Ensure or facilitate compatibility of subordinate communications system.

d. **JFC Communications System Responsibilities**

(1) Provide the overall management, compatibility, and protection of the communications system that supports assigned forces.

(2) Publish plans, annexes, and operating instructions to support the assigned mission and coordinate plans prepared by subordinate commands.

(3) If required by subordinate forces, request CJCS-directed transportable communications assets, to include USJFCOM's joint communications support element (JCSE) assets. The Service component commands have the overall responsibility for providing communications system support to their own forces unless otherwise directed. The JFC may adjudicate or assign subordinate commands the responsibility to provide the communications system support based on the situation and/or available communications system resources. In the network enabled environment, component

tactical communications system resources are considered for joint use and must be responsive to JFC requirements.

(4) Share information within the joint force and mission partners, which could include multinational forces, government, and nongovernment agencies to the maximum extent practical given legal, strategic, operational, and tactical considerations.

e. **Joint Force J-6 Responsibilities.** The joint force J-6 is generally responsible to the JFC for:

(1) Communications system issues and coordinating all procedures used in joint communications. This includes the development of communications system architectures and plans, as well as policy, guidance, and instructions for the integration and installation of an operational communications system. The J-6 exercises staff supervision of all communications system assets. This includes CJCS-directed transportable assets, automated information systems, collaborative information capabilities and tools and supporting environments, COMSEC, and networks necessary to accomplish the overall joint force mission.

(2) Ensuring subordinate component headquarters (HQ) establish network management and control centers. The J-6 establishes clear communications and reporting obligations between control centers. Each element of the joint force must have clearly defined missions and areas of control within the network.

(3) Coordinating cross-Service agreements between the joint force HQ, component planners, and the joint network operations (NETOPS) control center (JNCC). The J-6 establishes and supervises the operations of the JNCC to support top-level network control. The JNCC manages the tactical communications system and strategic communications connectivity as defined by the joint operational architecture.

(4) Reviewing all communications system plans prepared by subordinate component commanders. The J-6 facilitates the execution of all communications system actions to maximize support to the JFC and adjudicates any conflicts.

Detailed communications system techniques and procedures necessary to deploy and sustain a joint force are contained in the Chairman of the Joint Chiefs of Staff Manual (CJCSM) 6231 series, Manual for Employing Joint Tactical Communications, and annex K (communications supplement/instructions) of the JFC's OPLANs, OPORDs, or campaign plans.

f. **Associated Communications Elements Responsibilities**

(1) The **JCSE** is a rapidly deployable, joint tactical communications unit assigned to USJFCOM that provides contingency and crisis communications to joint forces. The JCSE is composed of Active and Reserve Component forces and is equipped

with a wide array of tactical and commercial communications equipment. The JCSE supports time-sensitive operations.

(2) **Theater Information Management (TIM) Cell.** The TIM cell reports to the operations community and is responsible for ensuring the commander's dissemination policy (CDP) is implemented as intended by the CCDR. The TIM cell is a full-time function collocated within the CCDR's joint operations center (JOC). TIM cell members take the guidance published in the CDP and combine it with late-breaking operational/intelligence information and network architecture/communications status information. The TIM cell works closely with the theater networks operations (NETOPS) control center (TNCC) in coordinating potential changes in either the Global Broadcast Service (GBS) schedule or DISN network changes to fulfill late-breaking updates in the commander's information dissemination requirements.

(3) The **Defense Information Systems Agency-liaison officer (DISA-LO)** serves as the principal interface between the joint force J-6 and DISA HQ. The DISA-LO assists the J-6 in coordinating, planning, executing, and evaluating the communications and computing components of the GIG. DISA supports the employment of communications resources at designated gateways and extends the DISN services to tactical networks. DISA contingency and support plans provide guidance for the request and termination of DISN services in the tactical environment. The appropriate DISA regional operational and security center supervises the allocation, routing, and restoration of channels and circuits to provide positive DISN support of deployed forces.

(4) The **regional satellite communications support center liaison officer (RSSC-LO)** serves as the primary point of contact in coordinating all ground mobile forces satellite requirements in support of the joint force. The JFC requests deployment of the RSSC-LO when needed.

(5) A **frequency management detachment** normally deploys with the joint force. The joint spectrum management element (JSME) coordinates, manages, and deconflicts frequency allocation and assignments supporting intelligence/operations/communications systems, including electronic warfare (EW), with the CCDR's intelligence directorate of a joint staff (J-2), J-3, J-6, and host-nation communications authorities.

CJCSM 3320.01A, Joint Operations in the Electromagnetic Battlespace, provides a detailed description of the JSME, its responsibilities, and reporting requirements. Also contains numerous samples of data call messages and planning checklists to assist deploying forces.

(6) A **J-6 operations officer** is normally assigned to the JFC's JOC to assist with communications matters.

(7) The **J-6 liaison to the information operations (IO) cell** coordinates all IA aspects of defensive IO. (See Chapter II, "The Global Information Grid," Chapter III,

"Joint Force Communications System Operations Planning and Management," and Chapter IV, "Network Operations," for additional responsibilities.)

CJCSM 6231 series, Manuals for Joint Tactical Communications, *provides a detailed description of each tactical communication element, its responsibilities, and reporting requirements. Joint Publication (JP) 3-33,* Joint Task Force Headquarters, *contains checklist questions to assist the J-6 in support of a joint force.*

   g. **The Defense Intelligence Agency (DIA) Deputy Director for Information Management** provides advice and recommendations about defense intelligence communications system matters to CJCS through the J-2. The DIA Deputy Director for IM serves as the joint community CIO for the General Defense Intelligence Program, which includes the Department of Defense Intelligence Information System (DODIIS).

Intentionally Blank

CHAPTER II
THE GLOBAL INFORMATION GRID

> *"Our information defines our decisions - Our decisions define our success."*
>
> **General James E. Cartwright**
> **Vice Chairman of the Joint Chiefs of Staff, April 2009**

1. General

a. **The GIG is the globally interconnected, end-to-end set of information capabilities for collecting, processing, storing, disseminating, and managing information on demand to warfighters, policy makers, and support personnel.** The GIG includes all owned and leased communications and computing systems and services, software (including applications), data, security services, and other associated services necessary to achieve IS. The GIG supports all DOD, national security, and related intelligence community (IC) missions and functions (strategic, operational, tactical, and business), in war and in peace. The GIG provides capabilities from all operating locations (bases, posts, camps, stations, facilities, mobile platforms, and deployed sites). The GIG provides interfaces to multinational and non-DOD users and systems.

b. **The GIG is evolving rapidly.** This publication focuses on doctrine and the general characteristics of the communications system portion of the GIG.

c. The GIG interacts with and provides connections to the national information infrastructure and the global information infrastructure. DOD's strategy is to empower joint forces with information needed to achieve successful military operations by integrating the seven components of the GIG described in this publication (see Figure II-1).

d. The GIG supports the JFC throughout the range of military operations. Offensive actions to affect an adversary's information environment must be routinely explored and analyzed as a part of the full range of alternatives during the joint operation planning process.

e. The GIG is designed to support the joint force and provides interfaces to mission partners in order to create a seamless access to information.

f. The GIG integrates DOD IT resources and considers the use of interagency IT resources to support US national interests and strategies. The GIG includes five fundamental characteristics: unity of command, common policy and standards, global authentication, access control, and directory services, joint infrastructure, and information and services.

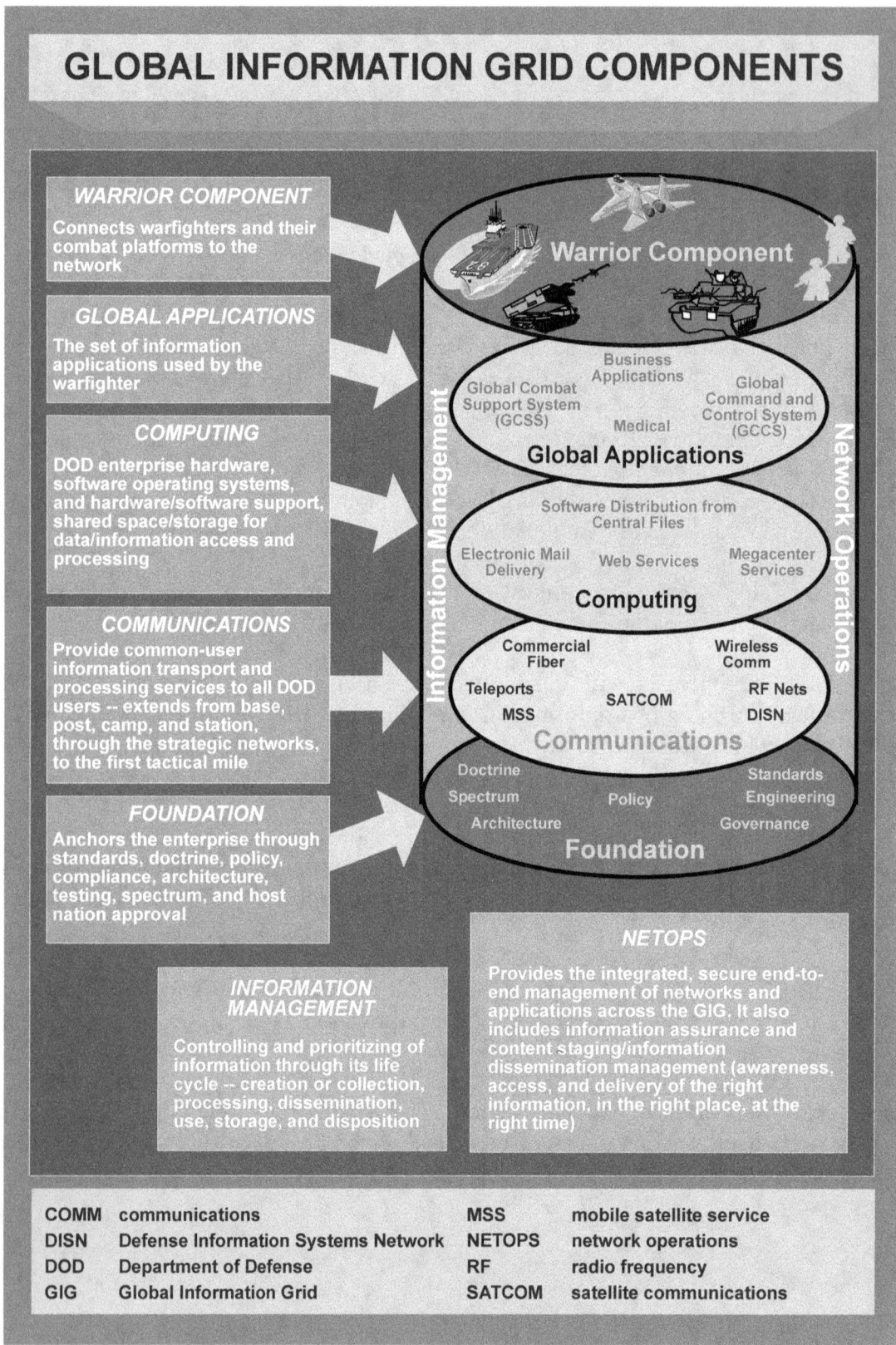

Figure II-1. Global Information Grid Components

2. Global Information Grid Characteristics

a. **Unity of Command.** This characteristic defines the necessary coordination and cooperation of supporting and supported commanders in relation to NETOPS of the GIG. USSTRATCOM has the mission to direct the operation and defense of the GIG to ensure the GIG is protected. The C2 framework embodied by the GIG also recognizes the authority JFCs need over cyberspace forces in support of joint operations.

b. **Common Policies and Standards.** This characteristic provides effective direction for data standards, information service standards, acquisition, certification, and enforcement to ensure seamless flow of information between all DOD and mission partner users and systems. Common methodologies and standards allow systems to be developed, tested, certified, and deployed with end-to-end interoperability.

c. **Global Authentication, Access Control, and Directory Services.** This characteristic describes a system that allows any authorized user with common and portable identity credentials to have access to information, services, and applications related to their mission and COIs. Additionally, means are put into place to ensure that tactically deployed users have alternate means of authentication in the event primary means are disrupted due to operations, enemy activity, or other causes.

d. **Information and Services.** This characteristic allows joint forces and mission partners timely assured access to required data and services in order to fully leverage the information advantage.

e. **Joint Infrastructure.** This characteristic provides a unified information environment that interconnects GIG users securely, reliably, and seamlessly.

f. **Enabling Capabilities.** The following enabling capabilities are derived from the GIG five fundamental characteristics:

(1) Improve DOD governance structure for the GIG with emphasis on unity of command and common policies and standards.

(2) Strict, unequivocal enforcement of common policies and standards across DOD.

(3) Availability of secure, interoperable communications and networks for DOD with global directory services, authentication, and access control.

(4) Availability of usable and reliable GIG enterprise services in a unified environment to all authorized users at all locations worldwide with emphasis on improved services to, from, and in the operational area.

(5) Establishment of a common joint infrastructure that enables information sharing across a diverse spectrum of operational requirements.

(6) Ability to ensure that the DOD primary mission essential functions can be completed regardless of the condition of the GIG or information environment through means such as enterprise resilience, continuity of operations planning, and network diversity initiatives.

(7) Survivability against threats cyberspace and physical.

3. Global Information Grid Planning

a. The planning of GIG support of the JFC is a fundamental activity in the contingency and crisis action planning process. Planning has evolved from the traditional determination of numbers, types, and locations of communications system elements to **a more comprehensive determination of the JFC's information needs.**

b. The complexity of joint operations and the finite amount of communications system resources may require the JFC to adjudicate or assign subordinate command responsibilities for extending the GIG's reach into an operational area. This is normally done in an OPLAN. However, in the absence of such a plan, communications are planned and employed as follows: senior to subordinate, supporting to supported, reinforcing to reinforced, left to right, between adjacent units as directed by the first common senior, or by the unit gaining an attachment. This order is more common to ground forces, but it may have application to space, special operations, naval, and air forces as well. These rules are generally followed except when sound military judgment dictates otherwise.

4. Global Information Grid Services Supporting Joint Force Operations

a. **Access Services**

(1) **Defense Information Systems Network Interface.** The DISN is the major element of the GIG (see Figure II-2). It has three segments: sustaining base, long haul, and deployed. It is DOD's worldwide enterprise-level telecommunications infrastructure providing end-to-end information transfer for supporting military operations. For the most part, it is transparent to the joint force. The DISN facilitates the management of information resources, and is responsive to national security, as well as DOD needs. It provides GIG network services to DOD installations and deployed forces. Those services include voice, data, and video, as well as ancillary enterprise services such as directories and messaging. DOD policy mandates the use of the DISN for wide-area network (WAN) and metropolitan networks.

(2) In concert with military and commercial communication segments that support DOD missions, the primary interface point between the sustaining base and deployed forces is called the **DOD Gateway.** The DOD Gateway includes entities formerly called the standardized tactical entry point (STEP) and upgrade called the Teleport. The DOD Gateway provides robust worldwide ground entry interface to SATCOM resources and GIG/DISN services. The DOD Gateway is designed to meet the

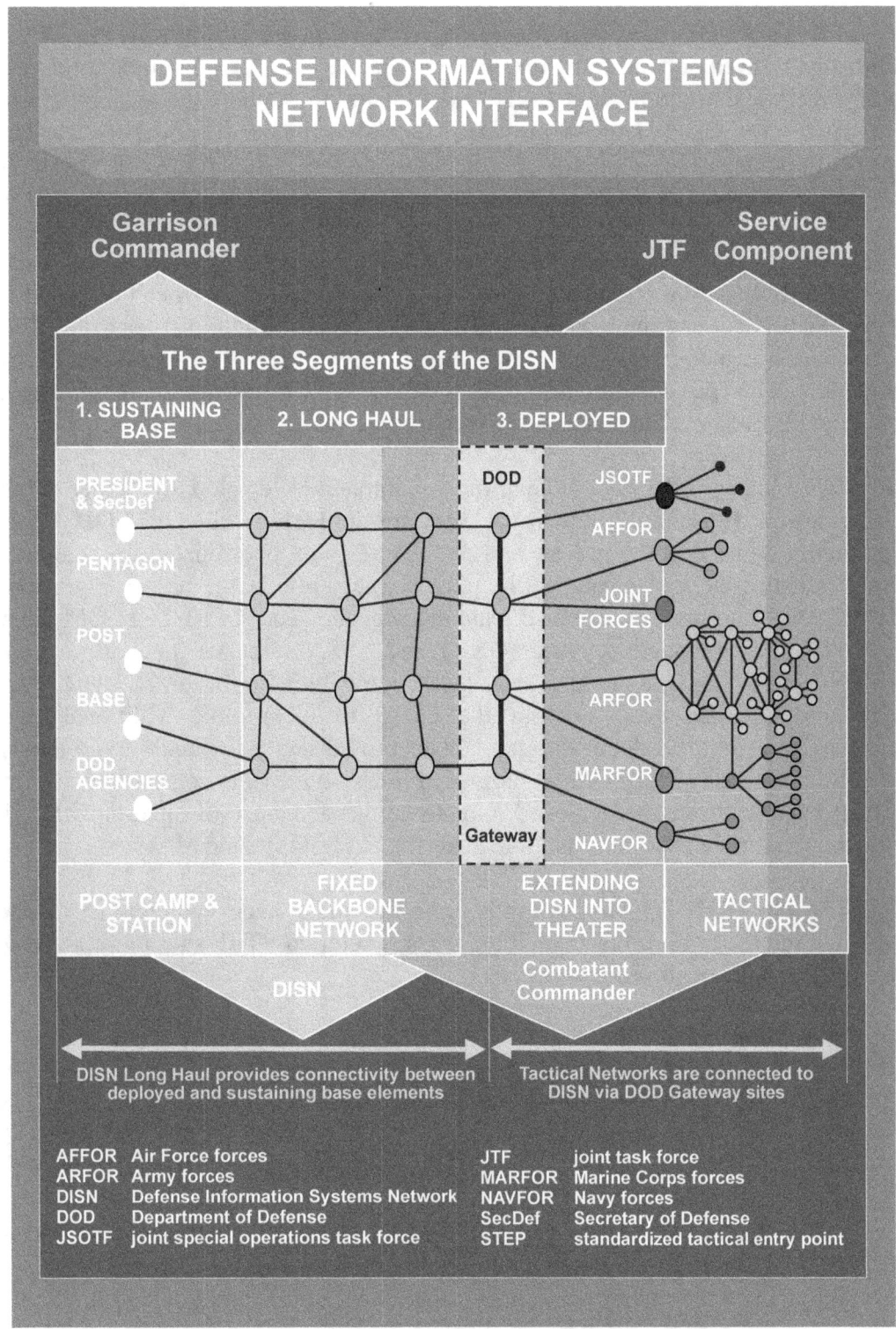

Figure II-2. Defense Information Systems Network Interface

requirement of the provisioning of pre-positioned, sustainable DISN services. An equally important result of this upgrade to the DISN has been the improvement and standardization (facilitating interoperability) of the JFC's access to the DISN.

(3) **The DOD Gateway program enhances the ability of the DISN to respond to the needs of the joint force.** Joint and Service-level operational users rely on both military and commercial SATCOM systems to support their communications requirements. The DOD Gateway provides predefined (tailored) support packages on a predefined timeline. This support is extended via common user transports and includes voice, data, and video services. These services are extended directly to deployed naval forces and to each component of a joint task force (JTF), if employed. Voice services include access to the Defense Switched Network (DSN) and the Defense Red Switched Network (DRSN). Data will include access to the SECRET Internet Protocol Router Network (SIPRNET) and the Non-Secure Internet Protocol Router Network (NIPRNET). Video services include access to DISN Video Services. It will also support the Joint Worldwide Intelligence Communications System (JWICS), a sensitive compartmented information (SCI)-level data, voice, and video services network.

(4) Although the DOD Gateway is implemented globally under a single executive agent, **JFCs and their staffs play an important role in DOD Gateway employment.** Entry point access and procedures are coordinated by the tactical communications system planners. DISA plays a major role in the planning process and utilizes regional contingency exercise planning branches and USSTRATCOM operated Global Network Operations Center (GNC) and DISA's theater network operations (NETOPS) center (TNC) to facilitate that interaction with the joint force. DOD Gateway (see Figure II-3) has evolved from the STEP to incorporate additional satellite connectivity through the Teleport program. This provides greater flexibility in the use of DOD and commercial SATCOM resources. Flexibility, in this sense, does not imply additional bandwidth for the deployed joint force, however use of quad-band terminals provide the joint force with more flexible means of SATCOM support.

(5) **The DOD Teleport expands upon the STEP access concept** (X band) and provides commercial and military satellite access at selected STEP sites to improve DISN service access to the deployed joint force.

b. **Voice Services**

(1) **DSN.** A standard unclassified voice network supporting DOD.

(2) **DRSN.** A classified voice network supporting DOD.

(3) **Enhanced Mobile Satellite Services** (e.g., International Maritime Satellite/Iridium Satellite). Commercial, portable satellite systems capable of voice and data transmission.

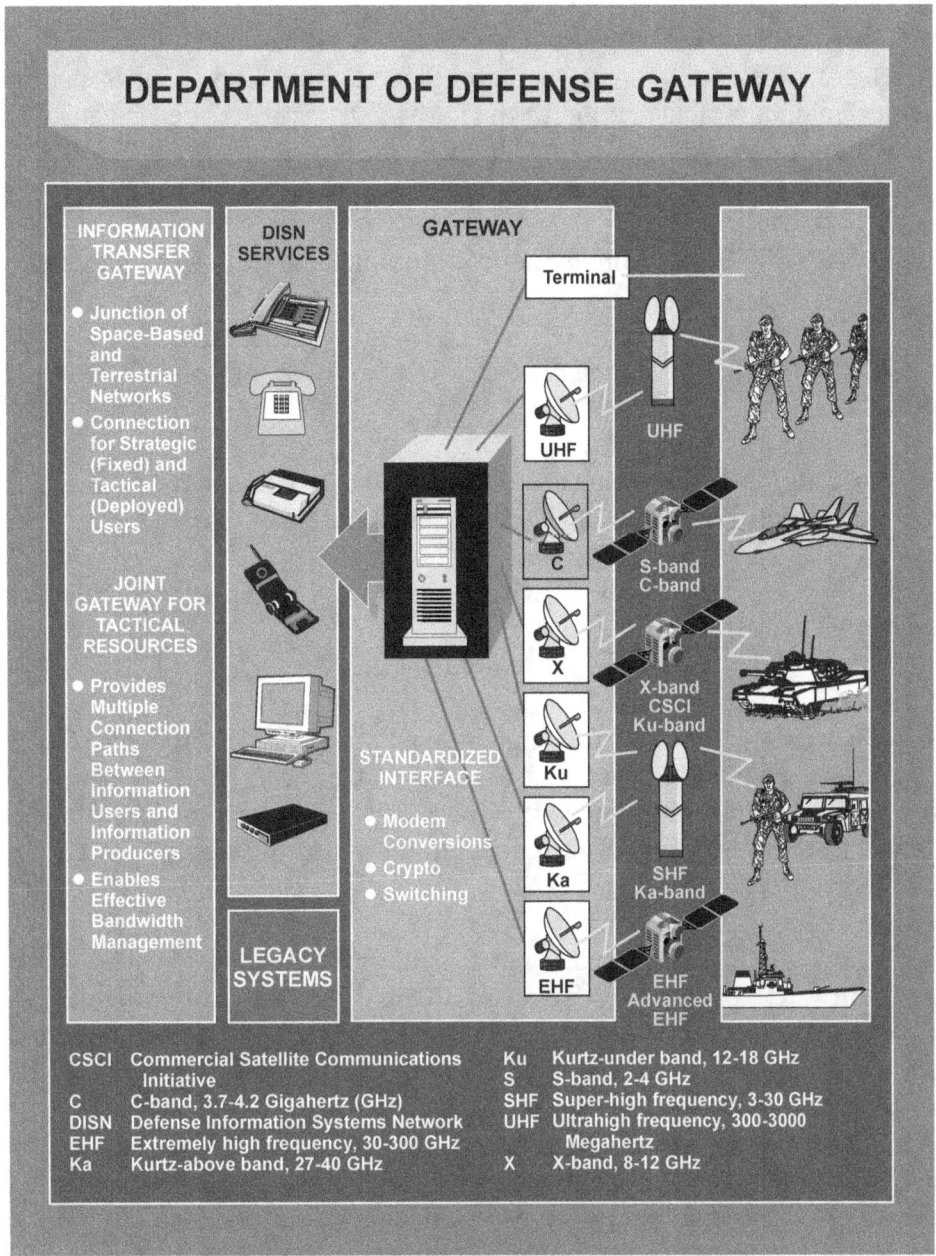

Figure II-3. Department of Defense Gateway

(4) **Tactical Voice.** Military specific switching system capable of operating in austere areas.

(5) Voice over internet protocol and voice over secure Internet protocol services.

c. **Data Services**

(1) The joint data network (JDN) is the network which carries tactical data link (TDL) and multi-sensor early warning information in support of joint operations.

Information is generally passed over the JDN in near-real-time. The JDN consists of the multi-TDL network, ground network, intelligence network, and sensor network along with other feeds such as the Joint Operation Planning and Execution System (JOPES). Effective design and implementation of the multi-TDL network are critical in managing the complexities of the electronic battlefield to improve the JFC's ability to engage hostile forces and prevent fratricide.

(2) **NIPRNET.** A computer network for unclassified, but sensitive information supporting DOD.

(3) **SIPRNET.** A computer network for classified information (up to SECRET) supporting DOD.

(4) **Coalition/Multinational WAN.** A computer network supporting the combined/multinational operations that may be unclassified or classified.

(5) **JWICS.** A computer network for classified information, including SCI, supporting DOD.

d. **Applications.** The Global Command and Control System-Joint (GCCS-J), the theater battle management core system (TBMCS), the Army Battle Command System (ABCS), the Net-Centric Enterprise Services (NCES) program, and the automated message handling system (AMHS) discussed in the following paragraphs are illustrative of applications.

(1) GCCS-J is a command, control, and communications system, consisting of hardware, software, procedures, standards, and interfaces to provide worldwide connectivity. The system uses DISN and must work over tactical communication systems to ensure connectivity with deployed forces in the tactical environment. GCCS-J employs an open system client/server architecture that allows a diverse group of commercial-off-the-shelf and government-off-the-shelf software packages to operate at any GCCS-J location. GCCS-J fuses select C2 systems capabilities into a comprehensive, interoperable system by exchanging imagery, intelligence, status of forces, and planning information. GCCS-J provides a robust and seamless C2 systems capability to the combatant commands, Secretary of Defense (SecDef), the National Military Command Center (NMCC), JFCs, and Service component commanders. GCCS-J offers vital connectivity to the systems joint forces and authorized mission partners use to plan, execute, and manage military operations. In addition to GCCS-J, the GCCS family of systems also includes GCCS-Army, GCCS-Maritime, TBMCS, Deliberate and Crisis Action Planning and Execution System, and the C2 systems portion of the Joint Environmental Toolkit.

(2) **TBMCS** is used by the joint force air component commander and other component commanders to collaboratively plan, direct, and control joint air operations in support of JFC objectives. This automated system facilitates the development,

deconfliction, dissemination, and execution of the air operations plan, air tasking order, airspace control order, and air defense tactical operations data message, and supports collaborative target management. The system provides full support to force-level and unit-level joint forces throughout all phases of military operations and is interoperable with other GIG systems to include GCCS family of systems, and GCSS-J/Command and Control Integrated Planning System. TBMCS is used by the US Air Force, Navy, and Marine Corps.

(3) **ABCS** is the Army's approach to automating its tactical C2 systems for component and joint operations. It is intended to give commanders from unit of employment to brigade/brigade combat team and below a common picture of the battlespace and to facilitate synchronization of combat forces in joint environments. ABCS consist of several major battlefield functional C2 systems intended to improve interoperability among Army, joint, and multinational forces. The subsystems include the Maneuver Control System, Force XXI Battle Command Brigade and Below, the Forward Area Air Defense Command and Control System, the All Source Analysis System, the Advanced Field Artillery Tactical Data System, and the Combat Service Support Control System.

(4) The current DOD tool suite for enterprise collaboration is Defense Connect Online (DCO). Fielded through the NCES program, DCO enables combatant commands, Services, and agencies with real time virtual collaboration capability using instant messaging, low-bandwidth text chat, and web conferencing. Instant messaging and web conferencing both include text-based communications, while web conferencing adds shared whiteboards, desktop and application sharing, and the ability to invite non-DOD personnel into collaboration sessions.

(5) **AMHS** is a multilevel secure, high mission assurance system for transmission of record message traffic in support of DOD.

e. **Video Services**

(1) **Defense Video Teleconferencing (VTC) System – Global.** A classified, closed video network capable of voice, image, and data exchange supporting C2 functions of DOD. It utilizes industry standard technology for robust interoperability to commercial systems as well as legacy DOD systems.

(2) **SCI-Level VTC.** A classified, closed video network capable of voice, image, and data exchange supporting intelligence, and C2 functions of DOD. (Note: SCI VTC is typically carried over the JWICS network.)

(3) **Commercial News Feed.** Commercial news feeds may be rebroadcast over DOD communications systems or received via a commercially leased terminal in support of C2 functions.

f. **SATCOM Services**

(1) SATCOM systems normally consist of three segments.

(a) **Space segment** (military or leased commercial satellites).

(b) **Terminal segment** (fixed and deployable terminals).

(c) **Control segment** (hardware distributed among control centers, satellites and terminals, and software to evaluate the status of the system stations and capable of monitoring, operating, and positioning the satellite, near real time allocation of satellite power, antenna orientation/nulling, and terminal monitoring and control).

(2) The DOD SATCOM architecture is flexible and adaptable (see Figure II-4). Current investment strategies attempt to find the right mix between DOD-owned and commercially-leased services, while balancing mobility, survivability, capacity, and assured access. **Emphasis today is focused on using SATCOM to support the deployed joint force by providing reachback to the sustaining base portions of the GIG.** In addition to these needs, SATCOM also supports a broad range of other missions and C2 requirements. SATCOM provides instant global reach to widely dispersed small and mobile forces; covers polar, open ocean, and remote areas of the world; and has a nuclear-survivable component with appreciable capacity. SATCOM supports a wide range of narrowband and wideband services for voice, data, video, and paging and is especially well suited for netted and broadcast services. SATCOM keeps en route forces and support systems supplied with critical information while deploying into an operational area. SATCOM can immediately tie sensors to shooters and provide beyond line-of-sight control of remote sensors and remote or in-flight weapons. SATCOM is also essential to the intelligence and diplomatic communities to provide worldwide transmission of critical intelligence data and sensitive diplomatic traffic over communications paths that remain under the direct control of the United States, especially during times of political tension or crisis.

(3) While it is clearly desired that DOD take full advantage (where affordable) of the commercial sector's capabilities and offerings, it is recognized that **not all communications needs can or should be met by commercial means**, especially in an unpredictable threat environment. There is broad consensus that there is an enduring need for DOD-owned SATCOM because military and commercial communications needs and uses are not convergent. There continue to be differences including the military need for nuclear survivable communications, plus antijam or covertness, with globally assured and immediate access, to including netted voice and data. In some cases, commercial SATCOM coverage is not available over the objective area or is not available for lease. Additionally, the military need to support rapid deployment of large infrastructure contrasts sharply with the relatively static commercial environment.

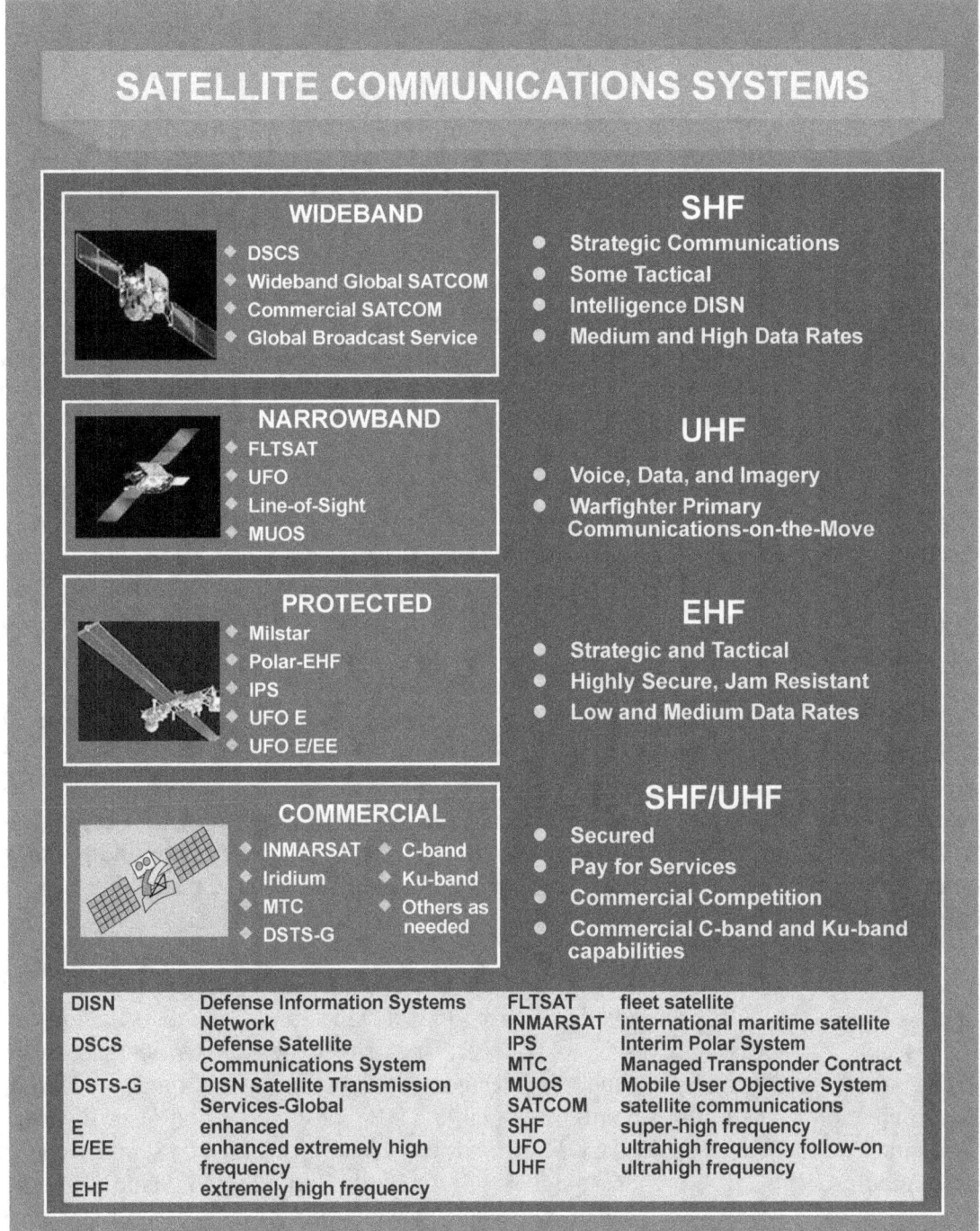

Figure II-4. Satellite Communications Systems

(4) However, **there is also a genuine need for commercial SATCOM.** DOD access to advanced capabilities of future commercial systems will provide faster access to new technologies or services. Commercial systems also provide additional capacity for surge demands. There is little DOD infrastructure needed to build or maintain access to commercial systems, which results in reduced acquisition, operations and maintenance,

and manpower investment. Along with these efficiencies, DOD benefits by only acquiring commercial capacity as it is needed.

(5) SATCOM resources are inherently flexible and well suited to supporting mobile and on-the-move operations. They provide the global reach necessary for DOD's global mission. Some of the advantages of the GIG's SATCOM architecture are the inherent ability to share resources over large geographic areas by individual satellites, the ability to provide worldwide (non-polar) or global coverage with a few assets, the capability to quickly service isolated areas, or rapidly extend new line-of-sight communications to mobile platforms. Currently, **the three main sub-architectural components of the GIG's SATCOM architecture consist of wideband, protected, and narrowband services** (see Figure II-4). Commercial services augment military wideband and narrowband services.

(a) **Wideband services** providing high-capacity and broadcast communications coverage to meet increasing demands for information include military-owned and commercially-leased satellite systems. Military-owned wideband systems include the Defense Satellite Communications System (DSCS), Wideband Global Satellite Communications (SATCOM) (WGS), Digital Video Broadcast – Return Channel Via Satellite, and the GBS.

<u>1</u>. **DSCS** provides a GIG transmission backbone of high capacity C2, intelligence and multichannel communications service for the CCDRs, Services, and agencies. Although not formally considered part of the architecture's protected communications capabilities, DSCS has a credible antijam capability with sophisticated satellite survivability features. The satellites are nuclear-hardened, providing secure voice and high data rate, long-haul, worldwide communications. DSCS satellites support deployed forces and ships.

<u>2</u>. The **GBS** is a DOD program for wide area broadcast of commonly shared information. GBS is capable of providing a wide range of video and/or data services on a broadcast-only basis to widely dispersed elements. Critical nodes are typically receiving terminals in support of designated C2 operations, but may include in-theater injection (transmitting) points if available. GBS provides a high-capacity near-worldwide military-owned SATCOM broadcast capability for dissemination of information products. The broadcast signals are transmitted to a large inventory of user-receive units worldwide. This capability makes possible a high data rate bit stream of video, data, imagery, and other information from high-powered broadcast satellites to a large section of the force structure and numerous warfighting platforms. The broadcast is transmitted from a limited number of fixed and deployable injection terminals controlled by the CCDRs, and managed by a broadcast management segment in each satellite field of view. The information being transmitted is collected from a myriad of sources and packaged for broadcast injection by the satellite broadcast manager or theater injection points. CCDR theater information managers nominate and monitor CCDR priorities, authorize user access, coordinate broadcast schedules, and allocate resources. There are three primary injection points operating to support the Pacific, European, and Central

Command theaters, along with numerous receive suites acquired by the Services to support operating forces.

3. WGS has evolved to become the replacement to the DSCS constellation. The primary function of the WGS system is to provide high-capacity communications services into the wide variety of large, medium, small, and mobile deployed force terminals. The system enables intertheater and intratheater communications for sustaining bases and dispersed users. US forces will use WGS to extend the ranges of their high-capacity data-transfer networks to other forces across the theater, to the sustaining bases, and to DISN points of presence.

4. **Commercial wideband** services are procured by DISA under such contract vehicles as the Managed Transponder Contract and the Defense Information Systems Network (DISN) Satellite Transmission Services - Global (DSTS-G). All Services and agencies are required to procure their long-haul communications services through DISA unless a waiver is granted by OSD. Currently the DSTS-G contract can provide:

a. Fixed satellite bandwidth.

b. Bandwidth and service management.

c. Leased earth terminal services.

d. Purchased earth terminals if approved by Army Communications-Electronics Command.

e. Global on-site earth terminal operation and maintenance.

f. Commercial teleport services.

g. US and foreign bandwidth and terminal licenses and approval.

h. Terrestrial interconnection services to support satellite service.

i. Host nation agreement-negotiating support.

j. Systems-engineering support.

k. First right of refusals and guaranteed reservations.

l. DISN common-user hub services.

m. Multiple location turnkey satellite systems.

(b) **Protected and survivable services** providing antijam, nuclear-survivable and LPD, intercept, and exploitation of communications capabilities including polar coverage are provided by military-owned and operated systems. Two of the key systems are Milstar and advanced extremely high frequency. A third system is the Interim Polar System (IPS).

1. **Milstar** is designed to support strategic and tactical missions through secure global communications that are jam-resistant and survivable with LPI and LPD. Milstar supports both single channel and multi-channel communications with low data rates from 75 bits per second (bps) up to 2.4 kilobits per second (kbps) (Milstar-I) and medium data rates up to 1.544 megabits per second (Milstar-II). Crosslinks between the satellites permit worldwide communications without the use of ground stations. Use of extremely high frequency (EHF) provides for narrow antenna beams for LPD and antijam capability. Additionally, EHF frequencies provide wide bandwidths for nuclear effects mitigation, as well as antijam capability. Both wide and narrow spot beam satellite antennas provide appropriate power levels for a variety of user terminals. The Milstar is the core DOD C2 communications system for US strategic and tactical combat forces in hostile environments. Additionally, small-scale EHF payloads are hosted on some fleet satellite and ultrahigh frequency follow-on (UFO) satellites to provide a contingency/surge capability for strategic and/or tactical users.

2. **IPS** provides EHF low data rate (75 bps to 2.4 kbps) communications to users above 65 degrees north latitude. A single satellite in a Molniya orbit provides 14-hour coverage to the polar region. Due to the nature of Molniya orbits, two satellites are required for 24-hour coverage. IPS supports combatant commands and NATO missions with C2, DISN, and essential targeting information.

(c) **Narrowband and mobile services** provide phone and data transfer capability for netted, mobile, hand-held, paging, and low speed broadcast. Some of the GIG's key systems in this category include military-owned fleet satellite communications (FLTSATCOM), UFO, and commercially available mobile satellite service such as international maritime satellite (INMARSAT) and Iridium.

1. **UFO and FLTSATCOM** systems provide low-cost user terminals that are small and lightweight, and can be used while on the move, under adverse weather conditions and in dense foliage. However, these ultrahigh frequency (UHF) systems yield low data rates, and are susceptible to both detection and jamming. Limited numbers of channel accesses available coupled with limited earth coverage satellite beams result in competition for access over wide geographic areas, requiring adjudication at the highest levels within DOD.

2. **INMARSAT** provides bulk use and pay-per-use alternatives that support information transfer requirements during both normal operations and periods of contingency or crisis. INMARSAT does not provide the survivability, LPI, or antijam capabilities required in tactical applications. It may be subject to electromagnetic interference (EMI), jamming, or intrusion.

<u>3.</u> **Iridium** (also known as Enhanced Mobile Satellite Services) provides secure and non-secure voice and data services to DOD tactical and non-tactical users. Although Iridium is a commercial SATCOM service, DOD has procured and installed an Iridium gateway which provides direct connection to DSN and NIPRNET services. DISA has contracts in place from which DOD and other US Government users can obtain service.

<u>4.</u> The **Trojan** network is the primary tactical extension of the JWICS network. The system consists of secure voice, data, facsimile, video, and secondary imagery dissemination capabilities. The system will receive, display, and transmit digital imagery, weather and terrain products, templates, graphics, and text between the continental United States (CONUS)/outside CONUS bases and deployed forces.

<u>5.</u> **Mobile User Objective System** is a narrowband military SATCOM system that supports a worldwide, multi-Service population of mobile and fixed-site terminal users in the UHF band, providing increased communications capabilities to smaller terminals while still supporting interoperability to legacy terminals.

g. **Aerial Layer.** The aerial layer provides additional communications capacity by using unmanned systems to host communications packages for continuous communications coverage of large geographic areas. The aerial layer integrates with the space and terrestrial network segments to enable advanced information exchange capabilities.

h. **Modeling and Simulation (M&S)**

(1) M&S of the communications system allows planners at all levels to design, analyze, and validate communication architectures to measure and assess the flow of information throughout various types of networks (data, voice, video, digital, and analog) and media (satellite, terrestrial, microwave, wireless, wireline, fiber optic, and others).

(2) M&S capabilities (such as the Joint Communications Simulation System of the DISA Program Management Office) have been developed to enable communications system planners and system developers to capitalize on the full potential of this powerful technology. These capabilities assist communications planners and analysts in a variety of circumstances including annex K (communications supplement/instructions) of the OPLAN development, validation, and execution; rapid contingency planning; network and configuration management; force-on-force wargaming; and new technology acquisitions. Simulation results provide quantifiable outcome predictions on planned or future communication networks or modifications to current networks.

5. Global Information Grid Framework Hierarchy and Structure

a. The attainment of IS requires unity of effort in command, control, and management of the GIG. As a practical matter, unity of effort is necessary due to the vast number of IT resources required to support worldwide GIG operations. The provisioning of GIG IT services includes all geographic combatant commanders' (GCCs') areas of responsibility (AORs), and all DOD users from anywhere in the world. The GIG supports DOD users that are deployed or operate from their home base. The GIG IT infrastructure, information services, data, policies, standards, and procedures must support the operational forces in all of their assigned missions. The GIG must be flexible and tailorable to accommodate changes required by the various CCDR missions. The GIG must also be capable of supporting operations at all levels of warfare from strategic to tactical operations. To enable the GIG to adequately support the operational commanders it needs to be centrally directed and coordinated to ensure all combat commanders receive a similar level of service and effectiveness. While centrally directed, the GIG will be operated in a decentralized manner.

b. IAW Title 10, United States Code (USC), Commander, United States Strategic Command (CDRUSSTRATCOM) implements the C2 structure to execute NETOPS operational priorities and has overall responsibility for global NETOPS and defense in coordination with CJCS and the other combatant commands. For operational effectiveness, CDRUSSTRATCOM provides unity of command for the GIG in coordination with CCDRs and DOD components. CCDRs will coordinate with USSTRATCOM through USCYBERCOM to ensure global impacts to the GIG are properly considered.

c. USCYBERCOM, a subordinate unified command under USSTRATCOM, focuses on military cyberspace operations. USCYBERCOM plans, coordinates, integrates, synchronizes, and conducts activities to direct the operations and defense of the GIG; prepare to, and when directed, attack adversaries in and through cyberspace in order to enable actions in all domains, permit freedom of action in cyberspace, and to deny the same to our adversaries. USCYBERCOM is a reorganization of existing DOD entities and authorities to improve DOD's ability to conduct cyberspace operations in an efficient and effective manner. The Director, National Security Agency (NSA) is dual-hatted as the commander USCYBERCOM. Previously, CDRUSSTRATCOM delegated operational and tactical level planning, force execution, and day-to-day management of the operations and defense of the GIG to Joint Task Force-Global Network Operations (JTF-GNO). The duties previously assigned to JTF-GNO under DISA and Joint Functional Component Command for Network Warfare (JFCC NW) under USSTRATCOM are the responsibility of USCYBERCOM. JTF-GNO and JFCC NW may be disestablished in the near future.

6. **Duties and Responsibilities within the Global Information Grid**

    a. **Office of the Secretary of Defense**

        (1) **Department of Defense Chief Information Officer**

            (a) ASD(NII), as the DOD CIO, serves as the DOD's principal staff assistant for IM, and consequently develops and issues the DOD information resource management strategic plan. **The DOD CIO is the GIG architect and is overall responsible for developing, maintaining, and enforcing compliance with the GIG architecture.** The DOD CIO provides recommendations to the Joint Requirements Oversight Council for the development of DOD GIG requirements and direction to the Joint Chiefs of Staff (JCS) for satisfying non-DOD requirements for GIG services validated by SecDef. The CIO will also consult with comparable IC authorities on matters of policy, implementation, and operation. Inherent in the CIO's architecture responsibility is the responsibility to enforce interoperability, IA, net-centric data sharing, use of enterprise services, and GIG program synchronization.

            (b) The **DOD CIO Executive Board** is the principal forum used to advise the DOD CIO on the full range of matters pertaining to the GIG. It also coordinates implementation of activities under the Clinger-Cohen Act of 1996, and exchanges pertinent information and discusses issues regarding the GIG, including DOD IM and IT. Chaired by ASD(NII), the board is composed of CIOs and/or senior communicators from the Services; the Joint Staff; the IC; USJFCOM; USSTRATCOM; the Director, Program Analysis and Evaluation; as well as the DOD Under Secretaries for Intelligence; Policy; Personnel and Readiness; Comptroller; and Acquisition, Technology, and Logistics. The primary mission of the board is to advance DOD's goals in the areas of IM, information interoperability, and IA between and among DOD components.

        (2) The Under Secretary of Defense for Intelligence (USD[I]) serves as the principal staff assistant to SecDef on the development and oversight of DOD IO policy and integration activities. In this capacity, USD(I), in coordination with ASD(NII), establishes specific policies for CND of the GIG.

    b. **Chairman of the Joint Chiefs of Staff**

        (1) Unless otherwise directed, communications between the President and SecDef and the CCDRs are transmitted through CJCS. CJCS exercises operational oversight over those portions of the GIG utilized for such communications.

        (2) CJCS is responsible for the operation of the NMCS for SecDef to meet the needs of the President, SecDef, and the JCS; and establishes operational policies and procedures for all components of the NMCS and ensures their implementation.

(3) CJCS also promulgates instructions and other guidance with regard to joint doctrine. These instructions include criteria and standards for assessing and reporting readiness of GIG assets.

(4) The **MCEB (Figure II-5) is a decisionmaking instrument of the CJCS and SecDef for determining corporate communications system strategy to support the joint force.** The MCEB considers and resolves issues related to the interoperability, compatibility, and integration of the GIG vision. The MCEB is chaired by the Joint Staff J-6/joint community CIO and composed of over twenty organizations from the Services and DOD agencies at the flag officer/Senior Executive Service level. The MCEB essentially coordinates GIG matters among DOD components, between DOD and other governmental departments and agencies, and between DOD and representatives of foreign nations. This includes operational guidance and direction to the CCDRs, Services, and agencies. The MCEB utilizes panels, which are functionally-oriented bodies with expertise usually in one specific area, to research and prepare issues for discussion and/or resolution.

(5) **The CCEB** is a five-nation joint military communications organization whose mission is the coordination of any military communications system matter that is referred to it by a member nation. The member nations of the CCEB are Australia, Canada, New Zealand, the United Kingdom, and the United States. The CCEB consists of a senior communications system representative from each of the member nations. The US representative for the CCEB is the Joint Staff J-6, who also chairs the MCEB. As the only joint combined organization focused entirely on communications system matters, it is positioned to provide leadership within the combined and joint environment. The CCEB defines an environment that optimizes information sharing and overcomes the disadvantages of transient coalitions. The CCEB seeks to achieve interoperability not just with technical standards and common procedures but also by spanning technologies and systems. The CCEB develops and seeks agreement on policies, procedures, and standards that enable the exchange of information in the combined environment including Allied communications publications (ACPs).

c. **Combatant Commanders**

(1) GCCs oversee and coordinate GIG planning and employment within their AORs. They exercise combatant command (command authority) (COCOM) over GIG assets assigned to their commands. They utilize the JTF-GNO, the TNC hierarchy, as well as Service component command TNCs as appropriate, and joint control centers. To this end, they collaborate with their respective Service components, DISA, DIA, and USSTRATCOM to create and maintain visibility over theater networks.

(2) CCDRs report on the readiness of GIG resources as a part of the Chairman's Readiness Reporting System consisting of the Joint Force Readiness Review, combatant command assessments, and plan assessments. The joint combat capabilities assessment (JCCA) provides the President, through SecDef and CJCS, a current assessment on the military's ability to execute its assigned mission in support of the national military

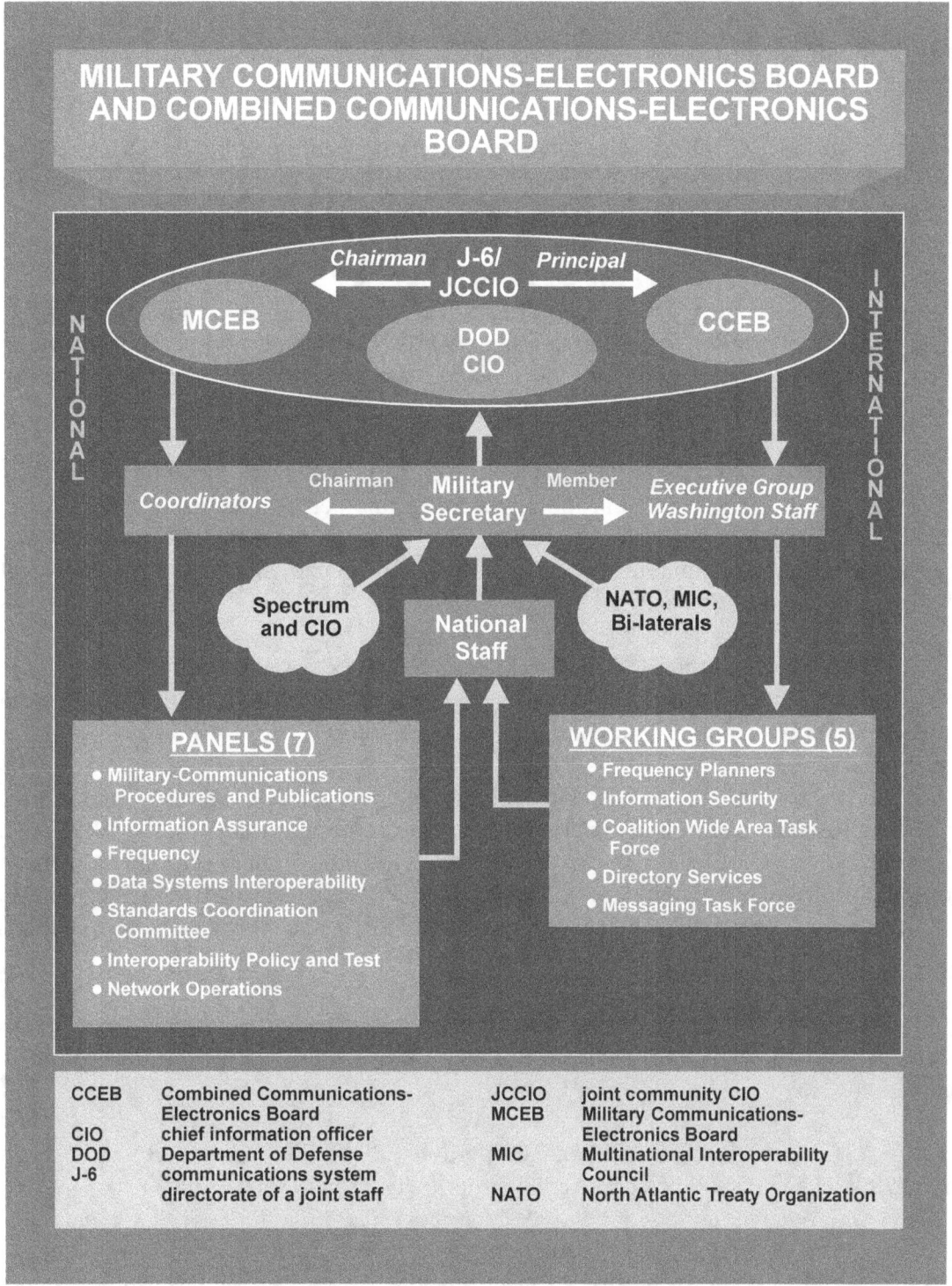

Figure II-5. Military Communications-Electronics Board and Combined Communications-Electronics Board

strategy. The JCCA assesses all functional areas, including communications system theater and strategic GIG infrastructure shortfalls, and limitations affecting the communications system.

(3) CCDRs identify, categorize (in terms of mission criticality), and assess risks to their mission critical assets (including information assets) via annex C (Operations), appendix 16 (Critical Infrastructure Protection) of their OPLANs.

(4) CCDRs validate the annex K (communications supplement/instructions) portions of their appropriate OPLANs periodically as a part of CJCS-sponsored or command-sponsored exercises. These tests will identify unresolved issues, verify operational procedures and interoperability, and provide joint training.

(5) GCCs identify their multinational interoperability requirements in the GCC's theater campaign plan. These requirements should be tested periodically as part of multinational exercises to identify unresolved issues, verify operational procedures and interoperability, and provide multinational training.

(6) GCCs identify their US OGA, NGO, and intergovernmental organization (IGO) coordination and communications system requirements. The operational area may have large a number of OGAs, IGOs, and NGOs. To promote unified action coordination may be necessary. Communications support, where needed, should be consistent with US law, regulations, and doctrine.

d. **Military Departments (MILDEPs) and Services.** IAW guidelines and direction from SecDef, each MILDEP or Service, as appropriate, has the following common functions and responsibilities pertaining to joint operations:

(1) Provide an interoperable and compatible communications system for the effective prosecution of military operations and plan for the expansion of the GIG to meet the requirements of DOD. In so doing, they will ensure that component-managed portions of all GIG programs are planned, resourced, acquired, and implemented IAW the DOD information management support plan (IMSP), the GIG Capstone Requirements Document and architecture, and DOD priorities.

(2) As GIG network providers, managers, or executive agents, extend GIG common services, to include voice, data, and video, to their organizations within the sustaining base.

(3) Ensure that Service-managed portions of the GIG are secure, assured, and interoperable, and that all personnel are appropriately trained.

(4) Provide frequency engineering and management within their respective MILDEPs and to optimize the use of electromagnetic spectrum by ensuring equipment use is planned so that sufficient electromagnetic spectrum is available. Operation of the equipment will be in compliance with national and international electromagnetic spectrum management and supportability programs, doctrine, and regulations.

e. Commander, United States Strategic Command

(1) USSTRATCOM has overall responsibility for GIG operations and defense in coordination with CJCS and combatant commands. **CDRUSSTRATCOM is responsible for coordinating and directing DOD-wide CND.** USSTRATCOM through its USCYBERCOM component executes the DOD mission. At the HQ level, USSTRATCOM responsibilities are to advocate for national requirements and standards, and in coordination with other CCDRs, assess and report the operational readiness of the GIG systems/networks.

(2) As military lead for CND, CDRUSSTRATCOM through JTF-GNO is responsible for the computer network incident reporting and developing coordinated response actions for a synchronized defense of DOD computer networks. This includes the development of defensive actions to deter or defeat unauthorized activity by coordinating release and distribution of IA advisories and alerts, and monitoring compliance of issued IA vulnerability alert. In addition, CDRUSSTRATCOM has authority to direct minimum-level DOD-wide information operations conditions (INFOCON) levels.

(3) CDRUSSTRATCOM has space operations authorities and responsibilities tasked by the Unified Command Plan. As the satellite communications (SATCOM) operational manager (SOM), CDRUSSTRATCOM centrally manages SATCOM to meet combatant command, Service, and agency operational requirements and strategic planning to support the SATCOM portion of the GIG.

For further information, see JP 3-14, Space Operations, *and CJCSI 6250.01C,* Satellite Communications.

(4) Additionally, CDRUSSTRATCOM develops, coordinates, and executes SATCOM policies and procedures, apportionment plans, constellation deployment plans, and satellite positioning and repositioning plans. CDRUSSTRATCOM also assesses how these various plans impact communications support to current and future operations and coordinates action prior to execution.

f. Joint Force Commander

(1) The JFC ensures an adequate and effective communications system is available to support the joint force C2 system. The JFC exercises this responsibility through the J-6.

(2) The J-6 then:

(a) Publishes communications system plans, annexes, and operating instructions to support the assigned mission. In so doing, the J-6 directs subordinate commands to provide communications system assets required to support the JFC. This may include assigning primary responsibility for communications to a subordinate or component command. The J-6 also assigns responsibility for lateral communications between subordinate commands.

(b) Provides overall management of the communications system supporting the JFC. As the forces deploy, the J-6 establishes a JNCC to establish network control and management within the operational area.

(c) Reviews and coordinates communications system plans prepared by subordinate commands.

(d) Provide for interoperability of the joint communications system.

g. **Joint Command Information Systems Activity (JCISA).** The JCISA is a theater-specific communications organization under the operational control (OPCON) of the United Nations Command (UNC), Combined Forces Command, Korea (CFC), and United States Forces, Korea (USFK). JCISA consists of active duty military and mission-essential contractors supporting the armistice and receives OPCON of all communications-computer assets during crisis and hostilities. During armistice and hostilities, the organization is organic to the CFC and USFK (C/J-6) and provides management, policy, plans, engineering, installation, network operation, maintenance, and system administration for Commander UNC/CFC/USFK's primary joint and combined C2 systems. The unit is staffed with personnel from all the US military Services; all the Republic of Korea military Services; and when augmented, is equipped with a wide range of communications equipment and capabilities.

h. **Department of Defense Agencies**

(1) Similar to other DOD component responsibilities, DOD agencies are also responsible for ensuring that their information systems environment is developed and maintained in a manner that is consistent with and reflective of the GIG architecture, and that agency-specific programs are planned, resourced, acquired, and implemented IAW the DOD IMSP and defense resource priorities. Those defense agencies, which are also part of the IC, are also subject to the policies and guidance of the IC CIO.

(2) **DIA** is responsible for the engineering, developing, implementing, and managing the Top Secret/SCI portion of the GIG including the configuration of information, data, and communications standards for intelligence systems, in coordination with the Joint Staff, Services, other agencies, and OSD. Included within this is the overall OPCON of the JWICS, a strategic secure, high capacity telecommunications network serving the IC with voice, data, and video services. DIA establishes defense-wide intelligence priorities for attaining interoperability between tactical, theater, and national intelligence related systems and between intelligence related systems and tactical, theater, and national elements of the GIG. The DIA exercises operational management of JWICS via the JWICS NETOPS center.

(3) The **NSA** is responsible for developing and prescribing cryptographic standards and principles that are technically secure and sound; development and executive management of DOD cryptographic hardware and software systems; and providing specialized support to the President, SecDef, and operating forces (e.g., national intelligence support teams and other special capabilities).

(4) The **National Geospatial-Intelligence Agency (NGA)**, as the functional manager for geospatial intelligence activities, is responsible for the development and evolution of the architecture for the National System for Geospatial Intelligence (NSG). As the functional manager for NSG, NGA actively communicates its architecture to members of the geospatial IC and promotes common standards and interoperability among NSG segments. The NSG is the technology, policies, capabilities, doctrine, activities, people, and community needed to produce geospatial intelligence in an integrated multi-intelligence environment. The NSG community consists of members of the IC, MILDEPs, combatant commands, and elements of the civil community. NSG partners include international entities, industry, academia, and DOD and civil community services providers.

Intentionally Blank

CHAPTER III
JOINT FORCE COMMUNICATIONS SYSTEM
OPERATIONS PLANNING AND MANAGEMENT

> *"Clearly, networking a force dramatically improves its capabilities for information sharing. This does not mean that all elements of the force are sharing information with each other all the time – but rather that all involved have the capability to share and access needed information. Sharing information is a prerequisite for a force to be able to develop shared situational awareness and to yield the warfighting benefits associated with enhanced collaboration and synchronization."*
>
> **Network Centric Warfare Report to Congress — March 2001**

1. Joint Force Communications Management Organizations

Joint communications system management involves the employment and technical control of assigned communications systems. Communications system management allows the planners to maintain an accurate and detailed status of the network down to the modular level. It combines centralized control with decentralized execution and provides effective and efficient communications system support for the JFC. Communications management policy and procedures are introduced Chapter IV, "Network Operations."

a. **Joint NETOPS Control Center.** The joint force J-6 must be prepared to respond to the JFC for all automated information system issues required to accomplish the overall mission. The JNCC is used to manage all communications systems deployed during operations and exercises. The JNCC, through component/Service control facilities, exercises control over many deployed communications systems and serves as a control agency for the management and operational direction of joint communications networks. Functional components and subordinate JFCs may establish a systems control (SYSCON) or NETOPS security center (NOSC) to serve as their single point of contact for communications system issues. The JNCC performs planning, execution, technical direction, and management over all deployed communications systems as discussed in detail in the CJCSM 6231 series, *Manual for Employing Joint Tactical Communications*.

(1) **JNCC Management Implementation.** When communications system networks are activated, planners and operators begin to monitor the status of the systems, networks, and nodes. User-detected system problems are reported to the user's immediate chain of command and supporting SYSCON/NOSC. They implement corrective actions to restore any outages. The SYSCON/NOSC directs the appropriate technical control facility to resolve the problem or coordinates with other technical control facilities and the user's chain of command to resolve the problem.

(2) The **joint network management system (JNMS)** is the system for providing enhanced network management capabilities to the JFC. The JNMS provides a CCDR and a potential JFC with an automated capability to plan and manage networked services, devices, and systems. The JNMS establishes the means by which network planning and management may be coordinated across all DOD communications system organizations.

b. **Services Component Management.** Components and assigned support organizations should designate a single office within their communications staffs to coordinate with the joint force J-6. Component communications system organizations should formulate and publish plans, orders, and internal operating instructions for the use of their communications systems. All components' technical control facilities perform network control and reconfiguration. For example, they change circuit paths, direct troubleshooting to resolve problems, and provide status information. Communications system management organizations need to account for traffic management in a packet-routed environment and circuit management functions.

c. The **joint information management board** (JIMB) serves as the JFC's principal organization to draft the commander's information dissemination policy and coordinates IM functions within the joint force. A JIMB should be convened during the initial development of the joint force IM plan and as required thereafter. It is chaired by that individual designated the IM officer. The JIMB should be composed of representatives from each staff section, component, and supporting agency, and operates under the supervision of the chief of staff, or other appropriate staff directorate, as best meets the JFC's mission needs. The commander or a senior representative provides direct input into the JIMB by detailing the commander's view of the operational environment management and its impact on information flow and IM.

2. **Joint Force Communications Planning and Management Structure**

a. **Executive Agent for Communications.** The SecDef or Deputy Secretary of Defense may designate the head of a component as an executive agent for specific responsibilities and authority prescribed at the time of assignment. This is done when no existing means to accomplish the DOD objectives exists and DOD resources need to be focused on a specific AOR.

b. **Combatant Command J-6.** The CCDR, through the J-6, provides communications system guidance and priorities to supporting commands and components. **The execution of theater guidance and priorities is through the TNCC** or the equivalent organization. To effectively do this, the TNCC must maintain near real time SA of critical communications system nodes. The TNCC works closely with subordinate JNCCs to ensure accurate, timely, and detailed reporting by subordinate and supporting agencies (see Figure III-1). The TNCC is a supporting operations center to the GCCs' JOC and is responsible for AOR-wide SA of NETOPS events and activities. It facilitates AOR-wide coordination of processes, such as authorized service interruptions and restorals, develops and conveys operational impact assessments of planned and unplanned NETOPS activities and events, supports development of courses of action (COAs), and ensures implementation of the GCC's orders and direction.

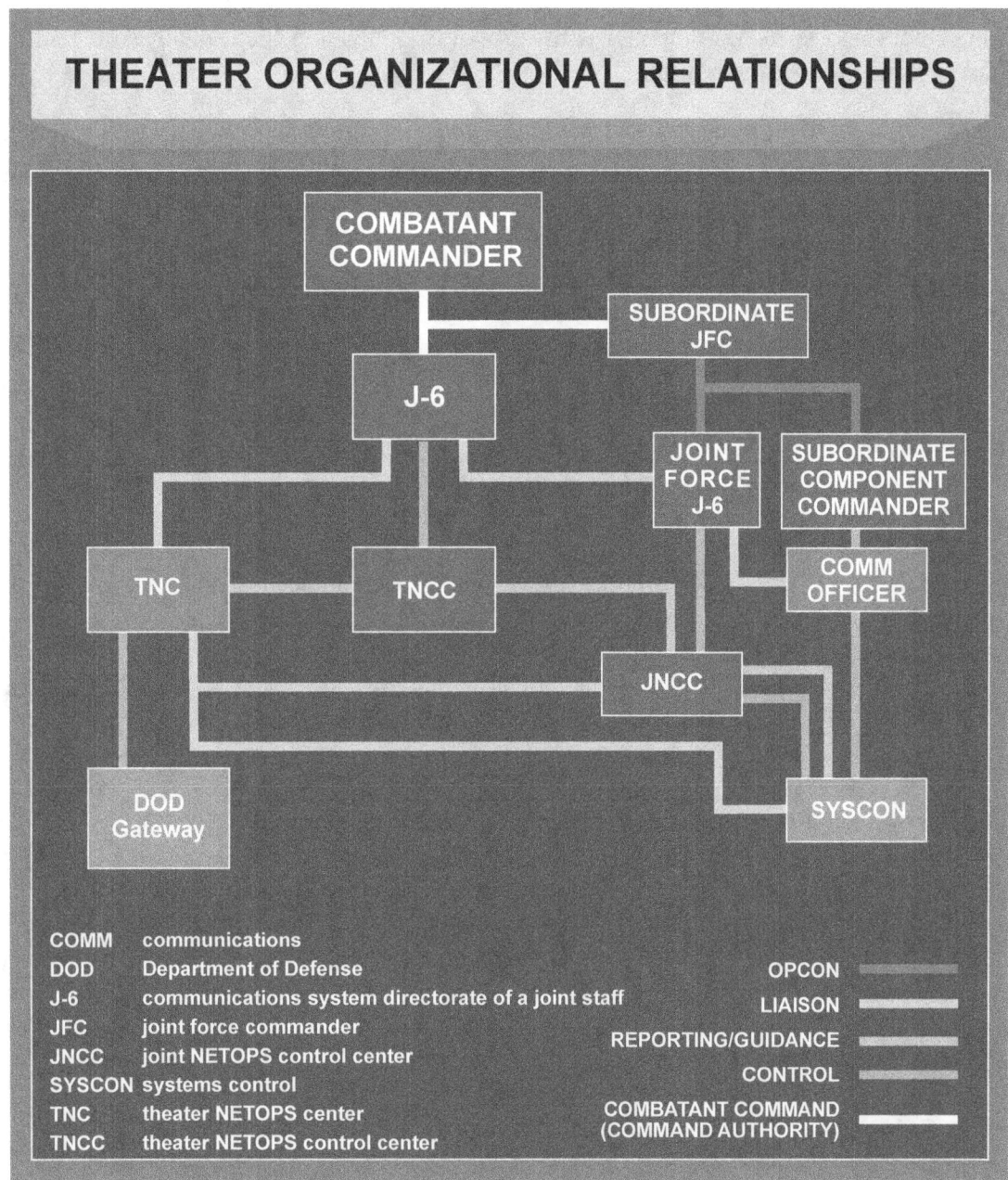

Figure III-1. Theater Organizational Relationships

c. **Joint Force J-6**

(1) The J-6 is responsible to the JFC for providing the communications system to support reliable, timely information flow in support of unified action. **The operational arm of the J-6 is the JNCC.** To direct NETOPS and retain SA, the JNCC requires timely support from a subordinate command's communications control center, commonly referred to as SYSCON or NOSC. Component, JTF, subunified command and agency NOSCs are responsible for assimilating and integrating NETOPS SA data of their respective operational areas. Each NOSC installs, maintains, and operates network

management and intrusion detection software and populates a local database to build a near real time view of their system.

(2) The J-6 assists the JFC in all communications system responsibilities. The J-6 establishes a JNCC to serve as the single control agency for the management and operational direction of the joint communications system. The JFC may task subordinate Service or component commanders to provide personnel augmentation to the J-6 to ensure the appropriate subject matter expertise exists within the JNCC. CCDRs and component commanders should designate a single office within their communications staffs to coordinate with the J-6.

For additional information, see Field Manual (FM) 6-02.85/Marine Corps Reference Publication (MCRP) 3-40.2A/Navy Warfare Publication (NWP) 3-13.1.16/Air Force Tactics, Techniques, and Procedures (Instruction) (AFTTP[I]) 3-2.22, Multi-Service Tactics, Techniques, and Procedures for Joint Task Force Information Management.

d. **Joint NETOPS Control Center.** The J-6 establishes a JNCC to manage all communications systems deployed during operations and exercises. The JNCC:

(1) Exercises OPCON and technical management over communications control centers belonging to deployed components and subordinate commands.

(2) Serves as the single control agency for management and operational direction of the joint communications networks and infrastructure.

(3) Performs planning, execution, technical, and management functions.

(4) Develops/disseminates standards/procedures and collects/presents communications system management statistical data. Functional components and subordinate JFCs should designate a single office within their communications staffs to coordinate with the JNCC.

e. **Subordinate Communications Units**

(1) Subordinate communications units must ensure reliable, timely information flow to both the JFC and their own commanders. Functional component communications system organizations should formulate and publish plans, orders, and internal operating instructions for the use of their communications systems.

(2) Normally, there will not be a conflict between support provided to the JFC's joint network and the respective subordinate commander's network. When there is conflict, a subordinate's SYSCON/NOSC cannot unilaterally decide the priority of support. It must coordinate with the JNCC to prioritize its activities. Additionally, it is critical that each SYSCON/NOSC provide timely, accurate communications system SA

to the JNCC. The SYSCON/NOSC can also coordinate with the JNCC to gain technical and/or interoperability assistance.

3. Communications Planning and Management

a. **Systems Requirements.** Essential elements of the communications system are driven by the mission and determined by the C2 organization and location of forces assigned to the JFC. Specific command relationships and the organization of units and staffs drive the interconnecting communications methods and means. The communications system must support and provide for assured flow of information to and from commanders at all levels.

b. **Joint Operation Planning and Execution System.** JOPES applies to the development and implementation of OPLANs and OPORDs prepared in response to requirements from the President, SecDef, or the Chairman. It specifies the policies, procedures, formats, and reporting structures — supported by modern communications and computer systems — for planning the mobilization, deployment, employment, sustainment, redeployment, and demobilization of joint forces. JOPES provides for orderly and coordinated problem solving and decisionmaking in two related but distinct categories — **contingency planning** and **crisis-action planning** — which differ primarily in the amount of available planning time.

For additional information on JOPES, see JP 5-0, Joint Operation Planning, and CJCSM 3122.01, Joint Operation Planning and Execution System (JOPES) Volume I (Planning Policies and Procedures)*, CJCSM 3122.03C,* Joint Operation Planning and Execution System Volume II, Planning Formats, *and CJCSM 3150.16B,* Joint Operation Planning and Execution System Reporting Structure (JOPESREP) Volume I.

(1) The joint planning and execution community uses contingency planning to develop OPLANs for a broad range of contingencies based on requirements identified in planning directives. The JOPES process is highly structured to support iterative, concurrent, and parallel contingency planning throughout the planning community to produce thorough and fully coordinated contingency plans in non-crisis situations when time permits.

(2) While contingency planning is conducted in anticipation of future events, crisis-action planning is based on the actual circumstances that exist at the time planning occurs. Within the context of JOPES, crisis-action planning responds to an incident or situation involving a threat that typically develops rapidly and creates a condition of such diplomatic, economic, political, or military importance that the President or SecDef considers a commitment of US military forces and resources to resolve the situation. Usually, the time available to plan responses to such real-time events is short. In as little as a few days, a feasible COA must be developed and approved, and timely identification of resources accomplished to ready forces, schedule transportation, and prepare supplies for movement and employment of US military force.

c. Communications system planners are responsible for ensuring that the organization's communications network can facilitate a rapid, unconstrained flow of information from its source through intermediate collection and processing nodes to its delivery to the user. Communications system planners should clearly understand the capabilities and limitations of all potentially available strategic, operational, and tactical communications systems and equipment, whether they are organic to Services and agencies, belong to non-US forces, are commercial, or provided by a host nation. Typically, the combined system will provide voice, data, and video communications. Building the communications system to support the JFC requires knowledge of the joint force organization, the commander's concept of operations, communications available, and how they are employed.

d. The J-6 is responsible for planning and establishing the communications system and the communications estimate of supportability (see Appendix B, "Joint Force Communications System Estimate Preparation Guide") during COA development and selection under the crisis-action planning process.

e. **Plans and Orders.** The J-6 is responsible for providing input to orders and plans, publishing guidance, coordinating communications system support and services, and gaining accreditation of joint force networks. The primary document for publishing communications system guidance is the annex K (communications supplement/instructions) of the basic order. After the communications system plan is developed and approved, the J-6 must ensure all networks receive appropriate accreditation. The J-6 may be the designated approving authority (DAA) and is responsible for accrediting communications system networks. The DAA will assign a certifying authority within each component. For all other networks, the J-6 must consolidate accreditation requirements, validate their correctness, and forward a consolidated network accreditation package to the next higher joint force J-6.

For more information on the accreditation process, see DODI 5200.40, DOD Information Technology Security Certification and Accreditation Process (DITSCAP) *and DOD Directive (DODD) 4630.05, Interoperability and Supportability of Information Technology (IT) and National Security Systems.*

f. **Communications Planning Considerations**

(1) **IA.** Achieving IA involves the employment of protection, detection, response, restoration, and reaction capabilities to shield and preserve information and information systems. CND is established to achieve IA and is focused on actions to protect, monitor, analyze, detect, and respond to unauthorized activity with DOD computer networks. Planning for CND to secure information and information systems is paramount to the success of the mission. It is a part of the defense-in-depth strategy.

(2) **Multinational Communications System Operations**

(a) **Multinational communications system operations may be composed of allied and/or coalition partners.** Coalitions can be composed of diverse groups of security and information sharing environments. Multinational forces may have differences in their communications system, language, terminology, doctrine, operating standards, and willingness to share information that can cause confusion and interoperability problems in an operational environment. Once the JFC establishes the specific C2 organization for a joint or multinational operation, the information exchange requirements (IERs) are established as communications system planning begins. Planning considerations include electromagnetic spectrum management; equipment compatibility; procedural compatibility; cryptographic and information security (INFOSEC); identification friend, or foe; and data link protocols. These and other considerations are further amplified below:

<u>1.</u> **Establish Liaison Early.** Effective communications system interface in joint and multinational operations demands the use of liaison teams. Their importance as a source of both formal and informal information exchange cannot be overstated. Requirements for liaison should be established early and to the extent possible, liaison teams should be trained and maintained for known or anticipated requirements.

<u>2.</u> **Early Identification of Communications System Requirements.** The demand for information often exceeds the capabilities of the communications system within joint and multinational commands. It is crucial that the JFC identify early communications system requirements that are external to the command or require support from national and/or host nation resources (e.g., space-based systems support, CJCS-controlled assets, JCSE, NATO standing communications system equipment pool, and electromagnetic spectrum). Multinational communications system planning must include the early establishment and incorporation of multinational networks. Resources need to be identified and planned for accordingly.

<u>3.</u> **Standardization of Principles.** Standardization of principles and procedures by multinational partners for multinational communications is essential. As US forces introduce new technology and become more network enabled, this area of concern is increasingly important. NETOPS, including activities conducted to monitor, control, and protect our networks, must be evaluated in the context of multinational networks.

<u>4.</u> **Agreement in Advance of Military Operations.** Multinational communications agreements should be made in advance of all phases of military operations with probable multinational partners. These should cover principles, procedures, and overall communications requirements (including standard message text formats, standard databases and data formats, electromagnetic spectrum management, and procedures for deconflicting frequency problems between multinational and civilian

organizations). Proposed multinational communications agreements should take into account existing treaty obligations as well as applicable status-of-forces agreements between the United States and other nations.

5. **US Interpreters.** The United States will provide or acquire its own interpreters to ensure US interests are adequately protected.

6. **Releasability.** This planning consideration pertains to US keying material and equipment, and multinational connectivity to US networks. The operational acceptability and disclosure or release of COMSEC to foreign governments for multinational use will be determined and approved by the National Security Telecommunications and Information Systems Security Committee before entering into discussions with foreign nationals. Commanders and their staffs should be aware of the limitations in sharing classified information with multinational partners, especially information from space platforms or other national assets. The JFC must plan for the additional time and coordination necessary to ensure compliance with established security requirements. The dissemination, disclosure, or release of DOD intelligence information to foreign governments for multinational use is approved only by DIA, the National Security Council, or the senior intelligence officer in theater, and should not be confused with disclosure of US keying material or equipment outlined in the previous sentences of this paragraph.

For more information on multinational operations, see JP 3-16, Multinational Operations. *For more detailed guidance on foreign access, connections, and COMSEC release see CJCSI 6510.06,* Communications Security Releases to Foreign Nations, *CJCSI 6211.02B,* Defense Information System Network (DISN): Policy, Responsibilities, and Processes, *and CJCSM 6510.01,* Defense-in-Depth: Information Assurance (IA) and Computer Network Defense (CND).

7. **Disclosure Policy.** Foreign disclosure officers should be appointed, trained, and certified early in the planning process at all levels of command directly involved in multinational operations. Their primary responsibility is to ensure common understanding of information that can be shared with multinational partners.

(b) Commanders and planners must consider several factors as they establish a multinational communications system architecture.

1. Rapidly determine what is shared, when, and with whom. Adapting a network to meet dynamic information-sharing rules advances modern warfighting operations in a multinational environment.

2. Understand the mission, intent, and concept of operations. Different phases of a multinational operation necessitate different and distinct levels of communications system support.

<u>3.</u> Have a comprehensive knowledge of the multinational structure and relationships.

(c) Communications system planning must be an integral part of joint force planning. Commanders and planners must:

<u>1.</u> Understand, expect, anticipate, and be prepared to deal with change.

<u>2.</u> Clearly understand the capabilities and limitations of available strategic, operational, and tactical communications system resources.

<u>3.</u> Ensure that communications to facilitate information sharing are established with non-US and host nation commanders.

<u>4.</u> Identify communications system requirements that exceed the capabilities within the joint or multinational force and coordinate (electromagnetic spectrum, equipment, or connectivity) any mitigating actions through appropriate channels when host nation support is required.

<u>5.</u> Ensure communications system capabilities and employment procedures for non-US forces are understood. To enhance multinational operations, at least three options for communications system assets and interoperability are available.

<u>a.</u> Use system-to-system compatibility to ensure interoperability. The United States may have to provide communications system resources to multinational partners to achieve this status.

<u>b.</u> Establish and manage an interface between incompatible communications system through a combination of interface hardware, software, and TTP to ensure interoperability.

<u>c.</u> Establish basic (voice and/or data) communication links and ensure unity of effort through the use of TTP and liaison personnel.

<u>d.</u> Although any multinational operation is likely to use a mix of these three methods, the wider the participation, the greater will be the reliance on the use of voice links and liaison personnel.

CJCSI 2700.01A, International Military Agreements for Rationalization, Standardization, and Interoperability (RSI) Between the United States, Its Allies, and Other Friendly Nations, *focuses on enhanced communications system combat capabilities for US military forces to communicate and share data and information with multinational forces.*

(d) The CCEB develops ACPs recognizing the importance of interoperability with the NATO Alliance. There are approximately 65 ACPs (basic and supplements) used by more than 90 nations. The CCEB is the only joint combined organization focused entirely on communications system matters. ACPs provide communications instructions and procedures essential to the conduct of common military operations. ACPs facilitate the use of available communications services and provide a basis for detailed procedural and operational publications on communications subjects such as frequencies, call signs, address groups, and routing indicators.

(3) **Support to ISR.** The communications system planned by the J-6 is the primary means through which ISR information flows to the JFC and throughout the operational environment. Communications system planning must be conducted in close coordination with the J-2 to identify specialized equipment and dissemination requirements for some types of information. Support provided by the communications system does not typically cover the collection and production of intelligence. The IC has a number of systems that are not part of the GIG. (See Chapter V, "Communications System Support to the President, the Secretary of Defense, and the Intelligence Community.")

(4) **Interagency organization, IGO, and NGO Communications.** Of increasing importance to joint operations is effective connectivity to non-DOD departments and agencies and NGOs and IGOs. Presidential Executive Order 13388 of October 25, 2005, directs DOD agencies and military Services to share classified and unclassified information with the interagency. In some situations, information sharing will also occur with multinational partners, intergovernmental agencies and nongovernmental agencies. JFCs need to identify interagency IERs and coordinate connectivity/access as required.

(5) **Morale, Welfare, and Recreation (MWR) Communications.** The J-6 needs to plan for local cellular and wireless services, which can be for official use or authorized MWR purposes. Because of electromagnetic spectrum considerations and security concerns, the J-6 should obtain a threat summary from the J-2 for adversary threats to communications networks in theater. Wireless networks in particular must be closely managed due to security risks.

(6) **Military Auxiliary Radio System (MARS).** MARS provides DOD sponsored emergency communications on a local, national, and international basis as an alternate communications capability. The program consists of licensed amateur radio operators who are interested in military communications. MARS has for many years provided morale, welfare, and official record and voice communications traffic for Armed Forces and authorized US Government civilian personnel stationed throughout the world. The combined three Service MARS programs (Army, Air Force, and Navy-Marine Corps) volunteer force of over 5,000 dedicated and skilled amateur radio operators is the backbone of the MARS program.

(7) **Support to Homeland Security and Defense Communications System Planning.** The DOD contributes to homeland security through its military missions

overseas, homeland defense, and support to civil authorities. The disparity of communications systems, use of allocated bandwidth (both civilian and military), and limited interoperable systems hinders the capability of collaborative incident management and response in the United States. However, standing JTFs exist that provide the C2 interface with federal, state, and local authorities. Interfaces include military web portals accessible by non-.mil servers, unclassified defense collaborative tool suite or similar commercial collaboration tools, JTF-owned deployable commercial voice switching, secure VTC in each governor's office, radio cross-banding so that land mobile radios, tactical satellite (TACSAT) radios, high frequency (HF) radios, and cell phones can communicate with each other, and links to national laboratories and other subject matter experts. United States Northern Command (USNORTHCOM) units include JTF-Civil Support, Joint Force HQ-National Capitol Region, JTF-Alaska, JTF-North, and USNORTHCOM standing joint force headquarters (SJFHQ). US Army North will also establish up to two regional task forces, as required. Additionally, each state adjutant general is building an SJFHQ with similar communications capabilities.

(a) Commanders and communications system planners need to consider the detailed planning and analysis to determine US-based communications system requirements in support of federal, state, and local agencies. For example, the JTF J-6 may need to rapidly gather information on the commercial communications infrastructure from the National Communication System and/or the National Response Framework Emergency Support Function-2 representative.

(b) The JTF J-6, when required and authorized, must bridge the gap between civilian, DOD, and OGAs to develop mission-oriented communications solutions.

For more information on communications system planning for the homeland, see JP 3-27, Homeland Defense, *and JP 3-28*, Civil Support.

(8) **World Wide Web/Public Internet.** Communications planning and execution is dependent upon persistent access to the public cyberspace. As the world's population increasingly gets its information from the public Internet, protected access to the World Wide Web is imperative for joint force communications, public affairs operations, and open source intelligence. This includes media and public perception analysis, global media SA, and the operation of public access websites for informing critical, worldwide audiences as part of a global information campaign.

(9) **Information Dissemination Management (IDM).** IDM balances a commander's information dissemination policy with the fluidity of the battlespace to ensure a JFC receives the right information, in the right place, at the right time, and in the right format.

(10) **Joint Network Communications Control.** Controlling networks is the art of solving communications problems by using logical and methodical procedures.

Network architecture is normally aligned with the CCDR's multitiered C2 structure — the combatant command J-6, the joint force J-6, and the staff equivalents of the joint force components and subordinate commands. This relationship can be easily extended to the multinational command elements, their communications control centers, and communications capabilities when a multinational force is formed. NETOPS is discussed in more detail in Chapter IV, "Network Operations."

(11) **SATCOM Planning and Management.** The goal of SATCOM planning is to ensure users have access to current systems and they are sized, deployed, and optimized to meet current and future SATCOM user requirements. SATCOM capabilities must be managed, monitored, controlled, and integrated with terrestrial capabilities to provide a comprehensive, seamless communications infrastructure. Communications planners and providers must have visibility into SATCOM and related network resources, for planning, implementing, monitoring, and sustaining communications support to forces within their operational area. SATCOM managers must have efficient and responsive methods for managing the complexities of multiple SATCOM payloads operating in many different frequency bands and network constraints or conditions while supporting diverse missions worldwide, as well as insight into threats, which would remove or negate those resources.

(a) **The three levels of the SATCOM operational management structure are oversight, system-level staff support, and 24-hour operations centers.**

1. The Joint Staff performs the oversight functions. These functions are accomplished primarily via the joint communications satellite center.

2. The SOM (USSTRATCOM), and the satellite communications (SATCOM) systems experts (SSEs) perform the staff support and management functions.

3. The global satellite communications (SATCOM) support center (GSSC) and the regional SATCOM support centers (RSSCs) are organized to perform 24-hour operations. These SATCOM support centers provide the global and regional direct support to users and their operations are closely integrated with GNCs and TNCs. The USSTRATCOM SATCOM C2 centers are responsible for satellite control and payload control execution.

(b) The organization with overall responsibility for SATCOM day-to-day operations is USSTRATCOM as the SOM. The SOM develops and implements standards, policy, and procedures for all SATCOM systems.

(c) Designated SSEs provide the staff and management support to the SATCOM COI as necessary. CDRUSSTRATCOM designates SSEs from within the component structure or delegates responsibilities to external agencies via a memorandum of agreement.

(d) The SOM, supported by the SSEs, provides the integrated SATCOM management infrastructure. In addition, the SOM is responsible for establishing GNCs and TNCs, as required, to provide support to combatant commands and other users. These centers are incorporated as part of the overall DISN management and control system.

(e) Tasks and Responsibilities

1. **CJCS.** Through the Joint Staff J-6, adjudicates differing resource requirements of the combatant commands that cannot be resolved between the CCDR, and CDRUSSTRATCOM, per CJCSI 6250.01C, *Satellite Communications*.

2. **CDRUSSTRATCOM.** As the SOM, performs all SATCOM apportionment, allocation, and arbitration. The day to day exaction of the tasks is delegated to the SATCOM operation managers at the GSSC.

3. **Commander, USNORTHCOM.** Advocate for non-DOD agencies conducting homeland security/homeland defense missions.

4. **Combatant command TNCC** or designated office. Validates and prioritizes all theater satellite access requests and adjudicates differing resources requirements of combatant command units within the AOR that cannot be resolved.

5. **Joint force J-6.** Validates, consolidates, and prioritizes all joint force satellite requests and adjudicates differing resource requirements of the joint force that cannot be resolved.

6. **GSSC Functions.** The GSSC provides the central operational focus for global constellation payload management. The GSSC performs the functions of the RSSC, described as follows, for those users not assigned to one of the RSSCs. The GSSC provides the central management for SATCOM accesses that require support from more than one regional center. The GSSC provides configuration management of the communications payload per USSTRATCOM direction as the SOM.

7. **RSSC Functions.** An RSSC follows the operational direction of the supported combatant commands and other users by defining requirements and allocating SATCOM assets. It analyzes scenarios, provides assessments, and assists CCDRs and their forces by translating OPLANs/OPORDs, annex K (communications supplement/instruction), and other planning documents into actionable requirements for SATCOM. An RSSC can also assist frequency managers and track, coordinate, and assist radio frequency interference identification and resolution.

(f) **Super-High Frequency (SHF) Requirements.** Wideband SATCOM terminals are a critical component in connecting the joint force into the GIG. These terminals extend GIG services to the joint operations area (JOA). The JFC establishes

SATCOM link priorities based upon mission requirements. If theater requirements exceed available resources, access is adjudicated per CJCSI 6250.01C, *Satellite Communications*. Naval forces afloat are assigned access by their respective RSSC as well and the combatant command TNCC validates and prioritizes these requests for access along with all other theater forces.

(g) **Commercial Satellite Communications.** Another method for US forces to access DISN services is to use deployable commercial SATCOM terminals, typically operating in the C-band, Kurtz-above band (Ka), Kurtz-under band (Ku). DISA manages commercial wideband SATCOM access through their commercial SATCOM team. Through this program, a user with combatant command validation can lease access to a commercial SATCOM transponder plus use of a commercial ground entry point (teleport or earth station) and long haul circuits to transport the information from the teleport to a DISN point of presence. While significant throughput may be available through commercial SATCOM, users need to be aware of commercial SATCOM planning considerations:

1. **Transponder Availability.** DOD must compete with the commercial sector for use of SATCOM transponders. Contractual limitations and flexibility can impact use. Planners must be aware of the current capabilities of commercial SATCOM vendors that may be contracted for within potential operational areas.

2. **Geographic Coverage.** C-band coverage tends to be fairly uniform between 76 degrees north and 76 degrees south due to the type of satellite beam used. Ku and Ka satellites, however, tend to use spot beams to narrowly focus the signal energy into populated (customer-dense) areas. Ku coverage now exists in blue water, but it is not global. Ku vendors are able to target coverage to specific areas to meet requirements of the customer base.

3. **Approval Process to Operate on Foreign Soil.** For a commercial SATCOM terminal to legally operate on foreign soil, certain agreements (host nation approval, landing rights for each type of terminal, activation fees, and frequency clearance) must be coordinated. The amount of time it takes to obtain these clearances varies widely on a nation-by-nation basis but typically exceeds six months. The J-6 consolidates and negotiates the technical issues of these agreements for the JFC. (In general, the J-4 is responsible for negotiating host nation agreements.)

4. **Haul-Away** (connection between commercial SATCOM and the DISN). If commercial SATCOM is incorporated into the communications system, connectivity (haul-away) may be required to connect the commercial services to DISN services. Typically, additional terrestrial services must be leased from the ground entry point to the nearest DISN point of presence. Because the installation of military-unique modems and/or multiplexers may be required at a commercial gateway, contract

agreements should specify the amount and type of services expected from the commercial gateway station personnel.

5. A gateway access request (GAR) and/or site access request (SAR) is required to obtain GIG/DISN services at DOD Gateway sites and usually accompanies the satellite access request. GARs and SARs are required to obtain services regardless of whether the satellite access is military or commercial. DISA provides circuit activation directives and DOD Gateway access planning guidance as required to support tactical user requirements when interfacing a DOD Gateway site. DISA also ensures that terminals and their assigned DOD Gateway sites are fully interoperable and the required access control is properly implemented.

6. **DOD Gateways.** DOD Gateway sites include STEP and teleport sites, commercial SATCOM gateways landing DOD commercial SATCOM leased bandwidth, and other gateways landing joint missions. The DOD Gateway provides a robust system for accessing SATCOM resources and GIG/DISN services. Joint and service-level operational users rely on both military and commercial SATCOM systems to support their operational communications requirements. DOD Gateway sites enhance access to military and commercial SATCOM resources, improve interoperability of Joint communications systems, and support seamless accessibility to the GIG by the JTF, deployed HQ, and deployed forces.

a. DOD Gateway sites are joint assets under the operational oversight and management of the JCS and USSTRATCOM respectively. Gateway equipment is available to CCDRs, Services, and agencies on a prioritized basis, IAW CJCSI 6250.01C, *Satellite Communications*. The Gateway supports warfighting forces and their supporting organizations deploying in all phases of a crisis. Access to DISN via a Gateway site provides the capability to rapidly extend services from any DOD location supported by DISN into the operational area.

b. The DOD Gateway system provides integration capabilities and contingency capacity. The system also provides the capability to connect deployed tactical terminals with other deployed tactical terminals in the same theater, including a seamless interoperability capability with the DISN backbone. DOD Gateway sites enable users in different operational areas to communicate by using one or more Gateway sites to "hop" from one operational area to another. Additionally, DOD Gateway sites enable customers using different portions of the satellite spectrum to communicate by crossbanding between frequencies (e.g., UHF to EHF, X-band to C-band).

For additional detail on SATCOM, see CJCSI 6250.01C, Satellite Communications.

(12) **Electromagnetic Spectrum**

(a) Critical to success in communications system support to joint operations is DOD electromagnetic spectrum management, which is a specialized area that relies heavily on systems engineering support and modeling to ensure electromagnetic spectrum dependent systems are mission ready and compatible within the intended electromagnetic environment. DOD electromagnetic spectrum management is the DOD business area of obtaining, controlling, and ensuring the effective and efficient use of electromagnetic spectrum through the development of policy, practices, and procedures. Joint electromagnetic spectrum operations apply the DOD electromagnetic spectrum management functions of electromagnetic spectrum operations, electromagnetic spectrum supportability, and strategic management of the electromagnetic spectrum. Each of these functional areas must abide by international, national, and military electromagnetic spectrum laws, regulations, and policies taking into account other existing and planned electromagnetic spectrum dependent systems as well as the environmental attributes of the intended operational areas.

(b) Strategic management of the electromagnetic spectrum is long-term planning of strategies, policies, practices, and procedures internationally and nationally for the expressed purpose of obtaining and maintaining necessary access to electromagnetic spectrum and capital investments of electromagnetic spectrum dependent systems.

(c) Electromagnetic spectrum operations consist of electromagnetic spectrum operational planning and frequency management.

1. Electromagnetic spectrum operational planning is the ability to proactively coalesce forces' electromagnetic spectrum dependent systems in support of the commander's mission, so that the mission can execute free of unintended friendly harmful interference.

2. Frequency management is the requesting, recording, deconfliction of and issuance of authorization to use frequencies (operate electromagnetic spectrum dependent systems) coupled with monitoring and interference resolution processes. Both national and international regulatory bodies require effective and efficient use of the radio frequency (RF) spectrum. US National Spectrum Authority, Title 47, USC, Section 151, The Communications Act of 1934, established separate control of federal government and non-federal government use of the RF spectrum. Under this Act, the only government agencies that assign and control the use of frequencies within the United States are the National Telecommunications and Information Administration (NTIA) and the Federal Communications Commission (FCC). The NTIA assigns and regulates frequencies for federal users. The NTIA governs all federal (including military) use of the RF spectrum within the United States and its possessions. The FCC assigns and regulates frequencies for non-federal users' respective boundaries.

3. Electromagnetic spectrum supportability is the combination of technological developmental engineering that focuses on physically matching electromagnetic spectrum attributes with desired system(s) characteristics toward the accomplishment of functionality and electromagnetic spectrum compatibility, from

system(s) conception to grave. Equipment (systems) certification and host nation coordination processes are both considered part of electromagnetic spectrum supportability. The goal of electromagnetic spectrum supportability is to provide functional electromagnetic compatible systems in support of combatant command missions.

(d) Both national defense electromagnetic spectrum management and joint electromagnetic spectrum operations, to varying degrees, apply elements of strategic management of electromagnetic spectrum, electromagnetic spectrum operations (electromagnetic spectrum operational planning and frequency management), and electromagnetic spectrum supportability.

1. **National defense electromagnetic spectrum management** are those activities carried out by the national defense electromagnetic spectrum management establishment (OSD, Joint Staff, combatant commands, MILDEPs, DOD agencies, and others) and is oriented toward the planning, programming, budgeting, and execution activities for electromagnetic spectrum within DOD, as well as national and international electromagnetic spectrum legal, regulatory, and policy coordination.

2. **Joint electromagnetic spectrum operations** are those activities in the joint warfighting arena carried out by joint electromagnetic spectrum operators (combatant command staffs, JTF, and others) whose objective is to successfully plan and execute joint or multinational operations across the battlespace. Assured access to the electromagnetic spectrum and electromagnetic compatibility are key enablers to joint or multinational mission success and the focus of joint electromagnetic spectrum operations.

(e) **Electromagnetic Spectrum Planning**

1. Electromagnetic spectrum management is the effective use and control of the electromagnetic spectrum. It is critical to national security in terms of global C2 of the nation's military forces. The rapid, ever-increasing growth of highly sophisticated weapons systems, as well as operational, intelligence, and communications systems, will increase electromagnetic spectrum demand (see Figure III-2). If this demand is not coordinated and carefully preplanned, it could have an adverse effect upon users sharing the available resources. Effective electromagnetic spectrum management is a building block of IO in defensive operations. It ensures necessary operations can be conducted with minimal unintentional interference (electronic fratricide) and without adverse electromagnetic environmental effects to ordnance.

2. Electromagnetic spectrum management boundaries extend beyond the realm of the joint force. Electromagnetic wave propagation does not stop at arbitrary boundaries, such as operational areas, or national boundaries. Therefore, coordination with all friendly and neutral parties vulnerable to EMI is essential. Interaction with the United Nations, host nations, allied/coalition nations, and nongovernmental entities may be required. Electromagnetic spectrum use by US forces, host nations, multinational

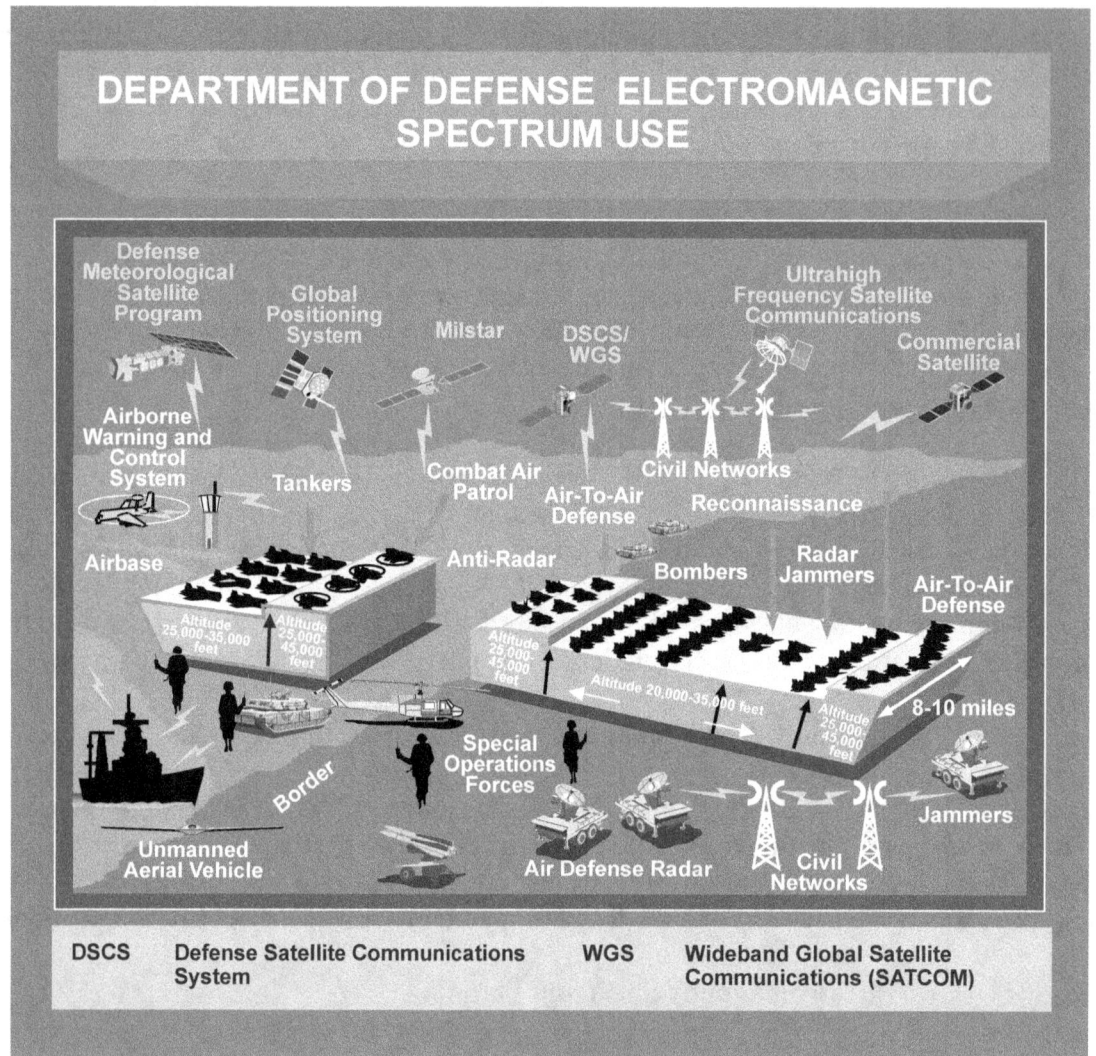

Figure III-2. Department of Defense Electromagnetic Spectrum Use

partners, and even an adversary, requires that planning for a military operation be timely, thorough, and comprehensive.

3. Each GCC is specifically tasked by the joint electromagnetic spectrum use policy to establish a joint frequency management office (JFMO). This office establishes procedures that authorize and control the electromagnetic spectrum resources in the GCC's command.

4. Command policy establishes how the electromagnetic spectrum is used in a specific operational area. Through established coordination procedures, the JFMO obtains clearance (or approval) from host nations for use of the electromagnetic spectrum. It ensures that assigned military forces are authorized sufficient use of the electromagnetic spectrum to execute their designated missions.

5. Each JFC establishes a JSME to accomplish these tasks in the operational area. The JSME is staffed with personnel from the Service frequency management offices (FMOs), GCC's JFMO, or a component's staff. The JSME must have joint trained electromagnetic spectrum managers experienced in joint electromagnetic spectrum use and knowledgeable of the electromagnetic spectrum requirements of the JFC's JOA. Electromagnetic spectrum management processes are critical to the success of the joint force and require close coordination with all the joint staff and relevant host nations. Electromagnetic spectrum managers at the Joint Spectrum Center and Service FMOs are available to help initiate these processes. The JFMO and JSME are tasked to implement these tasks to satisfy the needs of the military users and provide coordination with other entities. The JSME is responsible to:

a. Establish and maintain the common database necessary to plan coordinate, and control electromagnetic spectrum use. The database should contain electromagnetic spectrum use information on all emitters and receivers as appropriate for the operational area involved.

b. Analyze and evaluate potential electromagnetic spectrum use conflicts as part of the JOPES process, ongoing missions, and training. Support other staff sections with electromagnetic spectrum analysis to minimize electronic fratricide prior to or during operations.

c. Serve as the focal point for inclusion of electromagnetic spectrum use considerations in the JOPES.

d. Exercise frequency allotment and assignment authority. This may be delegated to facilitate decentralization and to provide components with the maximum latitude and flexibility to support combat operations.

e. Coordinate required military electromagnetic spectrum use with the electromagnetic spectrum authorities of host nations and if applicable the United Nations and NATO.

f. Develop and distribute appropriate electromagnetic spectrum use plans that include frequency reuse and sharing schemes for specific frequency bands.

g. Provide administrative and technical support for military electromagnetic spectrum use.

h. Prepare a joint restricted frequency list (JRFL) for approval by the J-3. This is accomplished through membership in the IO cell, or equivalent, and in conjunction with the joint force J-2, J-3, and J-6.

i. Update and distribute the JRFL periodically, or as required by changes in the task organization, geography, and joint communications-electronics operating instructions (CEOI), and transition through operational phases.

j. Receive, report, analyze, and attempt to resolve incidents of harmful EMI.

k. Assist in planning, coordinating and deconflicting electromagnetic spectrum use for electronic warfare activities through the joint force commander's electronic warfare staff (JCEWS) or the electronic warfare coordination cell (EWCC).

l. Assist and coordinate the resolution of electromagnetic spectrum use conflicts resulting in unintended consequences with members of the JCEWS and the IO cell or their equivalent.

6. Electromagnetic spectrum managers currently use a suite of automated tools that support CCDR, joint force, and component frequency managers. These tools include a frequency assignment database, proposed electromagnetic spectrum use templates, an equipment characteristics database, and a collection of engineering tools, to calculate the effects of current and proposed electromagnetic spectrum use on the electromagnetic environment.

7. EW activity. J-6 coordination and deconfliction for EW activity is critical because of its impact to the GIG. The GIG's increasingly wireless and space-based communication nodes are susceptible to interference from EW. Through the J-6, JCEWS/EWCC must coordinate closely with the combatant command's TNCC and designated JFMO. The TNCC will coordinate with the JTF-GNO to deconflict any anticipated effects of EW operations on the GIG.

See CJCSI 3220.01A, Electromagnetic Spectrum Use in Joint Military Operations, and CJCSM 3320.02, Joint Spectrum Interference Resolution (JSIR) Procedures. See also CJCSM 3220.01A, Joint Operations in the Electromagnetic Battlespace, for additional information about the functions and processes of the JFMO and JSME. It contains numerous samples of data call messages, planning checklists, flowcharts of processes, and descriptions of CCDR/joint force/component nets typically used.

4. **Communications Planning Methodology**

a. **Planning Group.** Planners within J-6 engage with their counterparts within the operations, intelligence, logistics, administrative, and policy communities to ensure proper consideration and inclusion of communications system support in mission execution. In addition, they plan the evolution of the communications system to support future operations. Communications system planning is divided into five areas: mission analysis, information needs analysis, interoperability, compatibility, and supportability analysis, capability analysis, and allocation of communications system assets.

(1) **Mission Analysis.** During mission analysis, communications system planners develop the communications system estimate and specified and implied tasks to be performed by operators and communications system personnel. The communications system estimate is the J-6's assessment of COAs that serve as the foundation of the commander's estimate, mission statement, intent, commander's critical information requirements (CCIRs), and concept of operations and support of it. Using foundational knowledge of the C2 organization and communications system capabilities, planners translate the concept of operations, concept of support, CCIRs, and environment into specified and implied tasks during each phase of operations. Tasks are developed for the deployment, implementation, operations, sustainment, modification, and restoration of C2 systems and networks to achieve IS throughout operations and support. Network management tools and C2 systems facilitate planning as well as SA.

(2) **Information Needs Analysis.** Communications system planners work closely with all functional communities to develop IERs. IERs identify products to be transmitted and received, as well as the throughput, quantity, and characteristics of those products. The communications system is tailored to meet the projected IERs. During military operations, planners conduct analysis to see if the mission, concept of the operation and support, CCIRs, and C2 organization necessitate the increase or decrease of the IERs, or new exchange requirements. Adjustments are made to the IERs as appropriate.

For a more detailed discussion of IERs, refer to CJCSI 6212.01E, Interoperability and Supportability of Information Technology and National Security Systems.

(3) **Interoperability, Compatibility, and Supportability Analysis.** Planners identify interoperability, compatibility, and supportability requirements and assess them against documented capabilities. When the mission permits, key interoperability and compatibility solutions will be validated before mission execution. Any shortfalls or deficiencies are assessed for operational and mission impact. In cases where operational and mission impact are too severe, the communications system planners determine whether it is operationally and technically feasible to resolve the problem in theater; if not, they request assistance from higher HQ.

(4) **Capability Analysis.** Based on mission analysis, information needs, interoperability, compatibility, and supportability analysis, communications system planners identify the C2 systems and networks that can support the OPLAN. Service component planners should be brought into capabilities analysis as soon as possible. Capabilities analysis is a daily assessment during all phases of the operation. In the joint environment, attention is given to the organic C2 systems and networking capability of deploying and in place units. Provisions must also be made for higher HQ connectivity to its subordinate HQ and component-to-component connectivity. Normally, a Service

component unit is assigned responsibility for communications system support at each HQ or other element, and a standard package of C2 systems and networks is provided. The standard packages are matched against operational needs. Listings of overages and shortages are produced for each location, major platform, and mission. Special attention is given to the time-phased force and deployment data (TPFDD) information and in-transit C2 for deploying units. In the end, a template exists that indicates the C2 systems and networks needed at each location, for each mission, and for each major platform.

(5) **Allocation of Communications System Assets.** After the template is developed, joint force and Service and functional component planners must examine all available resources and plan a tailored communications system. Planners engineer the various C2 systems and networks needed for the joint force. C2 systems and networks are centrally managed to ensure their proper performance. Organic communications units should be kept within their parent commands as much as possible. Some communications system units may be task-organized to meet the enlarged or reduced roles of higher HQ. Where units are collocated, planners should use the communications system assets of one unit to cover the other unit's requirements. Through all phases of the operation, planners should utilize commercial systems where appropriate. Communications system planners shall centrally plan and manage strategic and tactical SATCOM, electromagnetic spectrum use, and other C2 systems and networks to support:

(a) The joint force HQ.

(b) Service and functional components in the operational area.

(c) Connectivity to the DISN, commercial communications systems and networks, multinational communications systems and networks, and the Service communications system.

For more information on communications planning, see JP 5-0, Joint Operation Planning and Common Joint Task Force Headquarters Standing Operation Procedure Version 1.5.

b. **Planning Tools.** Automated planning and management tools are available to facilitate network planning, engineering, activation, and modification. These tools:

(1) Create/modify databases for communications system equipment and organizations.

(2) Define the network topology based on sites and by organizations.

(3) Create/modify subordinate unit tasks, responsibilities, schedules, and track performance.

(4) Conduct feasibility analyses using M&S.

(5) Create/modify and support distribution of communications plans and orders (communications annexes, the joint CEOI, JRFL, and communications service requests).

(6) Perform detailed network planning and engineering for a joint force network, including:

(a) Circuit switch planning and engineering.

(b) Asynchronous transfer mode planning and engineering.

(c) Data network planning.

(d) Video network planning and engineering.

(e) AMHS planning and engineering.

(f) Message switch planning and engineering.

(g) Backbone transmission system planning and engineering across the electromagnetic spectrum, to include the satellite ground segment.

(h) Radio network planning and engineering.

(i) Engineering plans and orders.

(j) Coordinate link and network activations/deactivations.

(k) Coordinate and integrate host nation communications system resources into the joint/multinational network.

(7) Graphically display network configurations and status changes in near real time.

(8) Provide the joint force access to communications system status information to enhance SA.

(9) Conduct performance analysis.

(10) Provide automatic capability to discover network devices and services, populate network management databases, and save each discovery for automated reporting of differences.

(11) Perform network device configuration/reconfiguration.

(12) Generate and process change orders.

(13) Perform automated fault management.

(14) Model, evaluate, and optimize proposed network changes.

(15) Assign and deconflict frequency resources.

(16) Perform automated communications propagation analysis.

(17) Support EMI resolution.

(18) Display regional defensive IO device status in near real time.

(19) Correlate IA events with respect to their impact on C2 systems and networks.

(20) Support electronic key management systems.

For detailed guidance of the communications system operation planning process, refer to CJCSM 3122.03C, Joint Operation Planning and Execution System Volume II, Planning Formats. *See also CJCSM 6231.07D,* Manual for Employing Joint Tactical Communications - Joint Network Management and Control.

c. **Development of the Network Plan.** Planners use automated and manual planning tools to integrate all communications system resources to ensure unity of effort, exploitation of total force capabilities, the fusion of information, and proper positioning of critical information. The network plan includes assignments of responsibility, hardware connectivity and configuration, software and application usage, and process functionality. The network plan provides the details necessary to bring communications system support together.

d. **Continuous Planning.** Planners must continuously update communications system plans until mission completion. Often, communications system support is first in and last out. As operations proceed through branches, sequels, and phases, planners must modify communications system plans as appropriate. The fog of war creates expected and unexpected contingencies that the planner must handle. Performance information on C2 systems and networks needs continuous analysis to identify trends and tendencies that may need to be changed during future operations. Communications system resources are continuously tracked.

e. In the absence of automated planning tools, planners must be prepared to use manual planning techniques.

5. **Communications Planning Factors**

a. The J-6 should be brought into the overall operation planning process early. The J-6 must understand the concept of operations and provide advice to the JFC during planning.

b. **The important factors for a communications system plan are feasibility and the adequacy of the plan to satisfy the JFC's information requirements.** A useful first step is the constant assessment of the communications system plan during the development process for its consistency with basic principles (see Chapter I, "Introduction").

c. Although communications system planning takes place in unison with the other planning elements of the joint staff, in reality, communications system planners must anticipate user requirements throughout all phases of joint operations. Every aspect of joint operations depends upon information to direct and accomplish the assigned mission. Plans and initial communications system support must be incrementally developed, deployed, and employed to meet the JFC's continually evolving mission.

d. Other factors to consider as the communications system plan is developed are:

(1) **Organic Communications System Resources.** As units are assigned to the mission, a quick assessment of available organic communications system resources is required. The objective is to keep organic communications system resources intact; however, there are situations where this is not practical. Throughout the planning process, the planner must track organic communications system resources within each unit and HQ. In a joint force scenario, where a commander of a Service force is designated the JFC, the Service force's organic communications system resources will be augmented by other Service components to facilitate the establishment of joint requirements.

(2) **Practical Communications System Support.** To the extent possible, communication planners should rely on joint standards and TTP to support the mission. In a complex network environment, unplanned changes and new approaches can have significant consequences if not fully tested and planned for. Training, exercises, demonstrations, and experimentation provide lessons learned and outcomes that identify what works and does not work. As the planning for current operations is ongoing, the prudent outcomes of brainstorming, exercises, training, demonstrations, and experimentation are employed in the current mission.

(3) **TPFDD Flow.** The JFC prioritizes the flow of units into theater. Communications system planners must monitor and influence the flow of communications system units, personnel, and equipment into the operational area to support the C2 of forces in theater.

(4) **Joint Reception, Staging, Onward Movement, and Integration (JRSOI).** Planners must arrange for communications system support during JRSOI. Limited organic communications system resources will be employed during this phase. Joint force planners coordinate with the Service components' planner for appropriate communications system support.

(5) **Incremental Building.** Because military operations seldom occur at the same location as the preponderance of our military forces, the JFC should expect planners to build the communications system incrementally. Most operations initially rely on SATCOM to move information between HQ and commanders. As the mission and assets allow, planners install voice, data, and video systems. Connections to the DISN and commercial networks become more extensive and robust as operations progress. Once the operation is complete, the communications system should also deactivate/redeploy in an incremental fashion.

(6) **Modular Packaging.** Based on the mission, the commander's intent, the OPLAN, the capabilities, limitations, and availability of equipment, and the communications infrastructure in the operational area, planners build modular packages to meet the commander's needs. Planners tailor these packages to existing conditions and link the individual communications system modules into a cohesive communications system.

(7) **Interoperability** should be achieved primarily by a commonality of equipment, software, and systems. Planners must know the capabilities and limitations of the other component communications system resources and must be able to integrate them into the joint communications system plan. The joint CEOI and COMSEC must be coordinated with Service CEOI/signal operating instructions and COMSEC must also be coordinated.

(8) **Standardization** should be evident in the planned communications system. Planners should ensure equipment strings and system configurations are standardized throughout employed units. The JFC's communications system requirements must not be compromised by uncontrolled, widespread use of nonstandard systems, protocols, procedures, or terminology.

(9) **Impact of Internal and External Changes to C2.** Planners must anticipate change and be able to respond in a timely manner to variations in the initial mission. The communications system plan should include a variety of communications system resources. Connectivity among commanders, HQ, and units must incorporate alternate routes and methods. A diversity of systems and alternate routes contribute to the communications system's flexibility, survivability, and responsiveness.

(10) **Commercial Capabilities.** Planners should consider and plan for the use of commercial systems. The availability of commercial communications system resources may offer an alternative means to satisfy the JFC's needs and may reduce the

number and size of deployed modular communications system packages. Commercial capabilities resident in the operational area may allow planners to compensate for tactical communications system resource shortages and meet the early information requirements of a joint force deployment. The use of commercial systems and networks may affect the planned mix of deployable communications system modules. Planners must ensure the deployed modular packages include sufficient capabilities to interface with commercial systems. Commercial capabilities may also assist in meeting the JFC's tactical communications system redeployment requirements.

(11) **Training.** The level of training of managers and operators of the communications system should be addressed. Of particular importance is training of individuals to integrate and operate commercial capabilities and networks with the JFC's organic capabilities. Additionally, communications system personnel need to possess adequate language skills to work with host nation and multinational forces. Language training needs to be available prior to deployment and in the operations area.

(12) **Discipline.** Communications system resources are limited. The JFC should ensure the information that moves through these limited resources supports necessary decisionmaking actions and overall mission execution. The mission and the commander's intent guide what information is provided to the joint force. The commander should provide additional guidance on what information is to be "pushed" and "pulled" to the joint force from the GIG. Long-established procedures such as "minimize" should be used and augmented to promote communications system discipline beyond just controlling the flow of record message traffic (e.g., VTC, e-mail attachment size, briefing slides, and others).

(13) **Timelines.** The goal of the communications system should be the acquisition, processing, storing, transporting, controlling, and presentation of information in real time, that is, as the event happens. The JFC should identify all critical information requirements. Priority lists that allow timely restoration of the most critical information should be developed.

(14) **Simultaneous Planning.** Planners should participate in the numerous planning cells of the joint force. Some of these planning cells are for targeting, future operations, IO, and others. The planning process for each of these cells is continuous and iterative. Communications system planners perform high-level planning to develop comprehensive estimates to design, engineer, implement, and maintain the communications system. Activation of communications system links and networks occurs when an OPORD is executed. During the execution phase of an operation, planners must consider the next phase of the JFC's operational concept and plan for its support.

(15) **Operational Limitations**

(a) **Connectivity.** The communications system should establish a level of robust connectivity that enables communication with the joint force, its subordinate forces, its higher HQ, and any additional reachback capabilities required. To the maximum extent possible, the hardware and software interfaces should be transparent to the system user. The continued flow of information should not depend on action by an intermediate user.

(b) **Range.** Range is a factor in connecting nodal points and networks. Equipment capabilities and the distance between nodal points must be considered.

(c) **Environment.** The communications system must be tailored to the environment, to include hydrographic, terrain, meteorological, vegetation, manmade, and cultural features. Such environmental surroundings determine the usable frequencies, output power, and location of communications system resources.

(16) **Collaborative Capabilities.** Planners should consider that a fully functioning environment of collaboration requires more than just **collaborative capabilities** that help participants share **information and knowledge.** A second component of this environment is **infrastructure** — the various information systems on which the tools reside and the networks that link these systems. The C2 systems, networks, and collaborative tools need **procedures** — based on accepted theory and practice and established to meet joint force needs — which regulate use in ways that facilitate collaboration. The full benefit of these capabilities is realized only with a fourth component — **users** who are trained to use the tools and systems and educated to understand the advantages and power of a collaborative information environment.

6. **Communications System Employment**

a. Communications system needs and capabilities of a small joint force with a limited humanitarian mission are vastly different from those of a CCDR with continuing multitasked, multinational-based combat missions. The phases of joint operations in a campaign are highly situation-and-mission dependent. Timelines between phases may be severely compressed. Phases may not follow each other in sequence; they provide a guideline for the JFC and communications system planner. Within the phases of an operation, it may be helpful to consider several activities that potentially affect communications system employment. For example, actions during an early phase may require mobilization and other predeployment activities to set the terms and conditions for operations. During predeployment activities, JFCs exercise flexible deterrent options and tailor forces for deployment. IA considerations are critical to all activities.

b. **Predeployment Activities**

(1) **During this time, the JFC is designated and forces are assigned.** CJCS warning and alert orders provide the JFC with guidance to initiate planning. The JFC issues a mission statement and commander's intent. Subsequent to the mission statement and commander's intent, the concept of operations is developed.

(2) **The objective** is to produce a plan to support the commander's intent, mission, and concept of operations and prepare initial communications system deployment packages to provide an initial operating capability that supports the operational plan. In addition, the planning of en route communications to support initial tactical entry may be required.

(3) **The method.** The communications system planner uses the planning methodology previously discussed to develop a plan to support the commander's concept of operations. To begin mission analysis and initial planning, the communications system planner must clearly understand the command relationships of the joint force.

(a) The basis of all communications system planning is an understanding of what joint and multinational forces are assigned, attached, or in support of the JFC. Collaborative planning, both horizontal and vertical, is a priority throughout all phases of the operation. The JFC communications system planner must involve subordinate and supporting organizations throughout the planning process. Automated aids, historical data, previous experiences, and intuitive judgment assist to develop the communications support plan.

(b) During mission analysis, the joint force planner works simultaneously with component planners and supporting defense agencies, such as DISA, to evaluate the existing communications infrastructure in theater to determine the strategic and tactical communications assets required. It is imperative that communications system plans properly sequence the deployment of assets to support the operational plan. The commander's C2 capabilities are limited by the capacity of deployed communications system assets.

(4) **The means.** This phase of the operation will rely exclusively on the existing commercial, strategic, and tactical communications infrastructure.

c. **Deployment Activities**

(1) **The plan is completed and published.** The communications system is expanded to provide improved information flow between the JFC and component commanders. As the system deploys, large pieces are extended into the operational area. Communications system assets deploy incrementally in support of the build-up in the operational area. Initial tactical communications are global, but can be insufficient in capacity if not properly planned, coordinated, and employed. The primary focus of initial

tactical communications system deployment packages is decision support to the on-scene commander and to provide the foundation for network expansion to support follow-on operations (e.g., lodgment expansion).

(2) **The objective** is to provide for the continuous flow of information between commanders during the initial phases of the operation and establish the base strategic and tactical communications system infrastructure to support follow-on operations.

(3) **The method.** Lift assets deploy the initial communications system capability. This initial communications system capability is composed of a modular package that provides the commander with voice, data, and video connectivity. The initial deployment package provides global connectivity as well as the foundation to build the remainder of the network incrementally. In austere tactical environments, the initial network is not robust and may be severely degraded when disturbed. Communications system support must include reliable, redundant capabilities that ensure the commander is always able to maintain C2 of component and supporting forces.

(4) **The means.** This phase of the operation relies on a mix of strategic, commercial, and tactical communications to support the introduction of forces into JOA. The JFC employs UHF SATCOM, military and/or commercial SHF SATCOM, EHF SATCOM, tropospheric scatter radio, and other military and commercial assets to support strategic and tactical long-haul communications requirements. The joint force uses other systems, such as UHF, very high frequency, and HF radio assets, to provide redundancy and support internal information requirements.

d. **Employment Activities**

(1) **Organization during deployment is the primary challenge.** The J-6 must maintain an effective organization that allows for rapid change. Although each subordinate command has responsibility to identify, schedule, and prioritize units and equipment for deployment, the J-6 needs to track arrival of communications equipment that supports key nodes. The J-6 needs to provide a centralized point of contact for coordination and status for deploying communications system equipment and personnel and ensure joint communications assets are included on the TPFDD. As units deploy into theater, they typically require tactical entry into the DISN via one of the theater DOD Gateway sites. Access to DOD Gateway sites requires close coordination and troubleshooting between unit and DOD Gateway technical control. Consequently, DOD Gateway activation support may have to be prioritized by the JNCC.

(2) Communications build-up during employment may be constrained by the deployment process. Both lift availability and unit preparation for deployment may delay immediate establishment of portions of the communications system. The structured approach to build-up of the communications system enables theater capabilities to rapidly provide initial communications, followed by a managed expansion of communications support.

(3) **Network Monitoring, Control, and Reporting.** One of the critical functions of the JNCC during employment is network monitoring, control, and reporting. Control of communications system functions consists of assessing the effectiveness of communications system operations, providing information, maintaining the currency of the estimate, and changing communications system operations in response to the evolving operational scenario. Network monitoring takes a macro look at the JOA from the J-6 perspective with the goal of ensuring optimum network performance. Reporting requires the establishment of performance measures and reporting thresholds, delineation of organizational relationships, responsibilities, and procedures (e.g., formats, media, timelines, and others), and identification of special interest systems, circuits, or communications system support for critical operational functions.

(4) The joint force and the Service and functional components continue a sequenced, balanced deployment. As assets arrive, they add capability and redundancy to the existing communications system. The JFC employs communications system assets to meet current requirements as well as support the planned operational scheme of maneuver.

(5) **The objective** is to produce a reliable, redundant, and robust communications system that supports the JFC's concept of operations.

(6) **The method.** A more capable communications system continues to arrive and expand as dictated by the mission, commander's intent, concept of operations, and to a certain extent, lift assets. Large capacity satellite, terrestrial switching, and transmission systems arrive during this phase of the operation. The J-6 through the JNCC establishes numerous alternate routes to increase the robustness of the network. Local area networks (LANs) are established at the joint force and functional component levels and are networked to the global WAN to increase information flow. As the system increases in complexity, more sophisticated systems are employed to maintain effective technical control over the expanding network. Throughout employment, the J-6 continues to plan the expansion and transition of the communications system to support the JFC's concept of operations for future operations.

(7) **The means.** The JFC relies on various systems including JCSE systems to connect to and expand other portions/services of the GIG into the operational area. Large capacity ground mobile forces and commercial satellite systems connect to the GIG with a mix of satellite and terrestrial systems to further extend the communications system into the JOA. SHF and UHF terrestrial multi-channel radios connect voice, data, and video via digital switches and technical control facilities. Maximum use is made of existing commercial and government systems throughout employment activities.

e. **Sustainment Activities**

(1) **The J-6 continues to refine and improve the communications system.** The communications system remains robust and flexible to support changes in the scheme of maneuver. An increasing concern during this phase is the quantity and availability of repair parts and consumables that are necessary for preventive and routine maintenance.

(2) **The objective** is to sustain and improve the automated flow and processing of information between the various commanders and develop plans to support any changes in the OPLAN.

(3) **The method.** Changes are made to the existing communications system as guided by the continuing mission, the needs of the commander, and the users. These changes improve the overall capacity of the system to move information seamlessly and transparently among components and national organizations. Less-than-perfect circuit design is corrected. As design flaws are corrected and the communications system becomes increasingly reliable, attention is turned to those actions that keep the system functioning. Plans are made for the redeployment of JCSE-controlled assets as other communications system resources are put in place. Continued attention must be paid to preventive and routine maintenance, adequacy of stocks of spare and/or repair parts, and consumables.

(4) **The means.** JNCC directs modifications to the communications system to respond to changing mission requirements and user demands or complaints. Technical control facilities take on an increasingly important role as they make changes to the established systems and maintain continuous service to the customers. Service organic and common-user transportation assets move consumables and repair parts to established repair facilities.

f. **Transition Activities**

(1) **Branch and Sequel Planning.** Changes in the JFC's mission, organization, or operations may require changes to the communications system architecture. Another source of change may be shortfalls in communications system support to operations, equipment or network degradation, and/or availability of a new communications system capability. JNCC future operations planners must actively monitor for these potential changes and develop branches and/or sequels to respond appropriately.

(2) **Transition Planning.** Although the original communications system plan will have a transition plan, the dynamic operating environment will make it necessary to review and redraft the plan. In many cases, although major operations cease, a residual communications capability is required, transition planning should consider both the transition of communication services to a permanent infrastructure and the potential deactivation of US communications system services. Frequently, services will transition to commercial or host nation provided communications system services.

(3) **Transition.** During this time, the J-6's priority is executing the transition plan. It is possible that a joint force for redeployment is standing or that there is a semi-permanent US presence left in and around the country. In this case, the J-6 needs to liaison closely with the newly designated organization to conduct a smooth transition of responsibilities and control.

g. **Termination or Post-Conflict Activities**

(1) **The planner must anticipate the termination of combat operations or the transition to post-conflict operations.** This stage of planning and execution must establish the basis for redeployment operations and continue to meet the communications system needs of supported commands.

(2) **The objective** is to monitor the transition of communications system assets to meet changing operational requirements and ensure continuous support for the joint force.

(3) **The method.** It is imperative that the communications system is not reduced too rapidly so it may continue to support the JFC's follow-on mission. The planner must retain a flexible, dynamic network to meet rapidly changing mission requirements. As subordinate elements reposition or are assigned new missions, the JNCC adjusts the network to provide continuous capabilities. Reliance on satellite systems may grow during this period as more forces prepare to redeploy while the JOA remains the same. The planner employs redundant capabilities such as UHF TACSAT to ensure the continuous flow of information across the operational area. The planner must anticipate an increased reliance on the local commercial infrastructure to facilitate host nation coordination.

(4) **The means.** As with the previous phases, this phase of the operation relies on various systems to connect to and expand the GIG into the operational area. Large-capacity satellite systems continue to provide connectivity to other parts/services of the GIG to dispersed forces throughout the operational area. Systems such as UHF TACSAT or host nation communications provide redundant capabilities throughout the operational area.

h. **Redeployment Activities**

(1) As during predeployment activities, **planning is the most important part of the redeployment.** The communications system must continue to provide information flow to the commanders, even as it purposefully disengages and large components of the network are removed for redeployment.

(2) **The objective** is to redeploy unnecessary systems and continue to provide communications support for the JFC and those multinational and functional component

forces remaining in the operational area. The JNCC must focus on retaining and transitioning network control until the joint network no longer exists. A JNCC should remain standing whenever either of two conditions exist: there is a portion of the operational joint network where more than one subordinate command requires the communications support from another subordinate command; or there exists one or more deployed joint organizations which require communications system support. During this time, the JNCC must ensure all units follow J-6 guidelines regarding deactivation of their respective communications system resources. To ensure an orderly deactivation and continued support of minimum network services, supporting components/commands/units coordinate with the JNCC prior to deactivating DISN services.

(3) **The method.** While amount of sustainment capability and the number of redundant systems will decrease, the J-6 must maintain some communications system capabilities until the JFC no longer requires them. In the final days of redeployment activities, the communications system may look very similar to the system originally deployed.

(4) **The means.** The original commercial and government infrastructure should support as much of the communications system redeployment as possible. Lacking such an infrastructure, the last systems to redeploy are typically the mobile and easily transportable assets; such as UHF single-channel and small SHF satellite terminals.

CHAPTER IV
NETWORK OPERATIONS

"Network centric warfare posits merging our warfighting capabilities into a seamless, joint warfighting force. It capitalizes on the trust we place in our junior and noncommissioned officers. As information moves down echelon, so does combat power, meaning smaller joint force packages wield greater combat power."

Vice Admiral Arthur K. Cebrowski, US Navy
Retired 15, January 2004

1. Introduction

a. NETOPS provides integrated network visibility and end-to-end management of networks, global applications, and services across the GIG, establishing, maintaining, and protecting DOD's networks that are a part of cyberspace. Network visibility enables commanders to manage their networks as they would other combat systems. Effective NETOPS culminates in assured service to the joint force facilitating network enabled operations. Visibility of NETOPS across the GIG is critical to operational transparency and resource efficiencies. Shared SA for all aspects of NETOPS along with coordination between stakeholders on potential events allow GCCs to be aware of network actions taking place in their AORs. GCCs will have the final authority over network activities in their AOR during contingencies.

(1) NETOPS is the responsibility of all DOD components. In accordance with the Unified Command Plan, the mission assigned to CDRUSSTRATCOM is to plan, integrate, and coordinate DOD global network operations by directing GIG operations and defense.

(2) A common set of NETOPS mission-driven metrics, measurements, and reporting criteria is used to assess GIG operating performance and to determine the mission impact of service degradations or outages.

b. The NETOPS mission is to operate and defend the GIG. Unlike many missions that are deemed successful at a defined completion date, the NETOPS mission is perpetual, requiring continual support to be successful. NETOPS provides a suite of assured network enabled services in support of DOD's full spectrum of warfighting, intelligence, and business missions throughout the GIG.

c. The effectiveness of NETOPS is measured in terms of availability and reliability of network enabled services, across all areas of interest, in adherence to agreed-upon service levels and policies. The method for service assurance in a net enabled collaborative environment is to establish operational thresholds, compliance monitoring, and a clear understanding of the capabilities between enterprise service/resource providers and consumers through service level agreements (SLAs). Proper instrumentation of the GIG enables monitoring of adherence to these SLAs, as well as enables timely decisionmaking, service prioritization, resource allocation, root cause, and mission impact assessment. SLAs are used to facilitate the transfer of funds between organizations to perform tasks. Operational level agreements are used to coordinate actions between organizations when funds do not need to be transferred. A key factor in NETOPS is the readiness posture of DOD, the combatant commands, Services, DOD agencies, and the GIG. All mission relevant factors must be included in assessment of readiness of the DOD components to perform their assigned missions and functions. Understanding of current readiness is dependent upon the current situation. Therefore, global and local SA is the key to achieving the goals of NETOPS.

d. The purpose of NETOPS is assured system and network availability, assured information protection, and assured information delivery, which protect and maintain freedom of action for DOD missions within cyberspace. Integration of the NETOPS essential tasks must be performed at the strategic, operational, and tactical levels and across all DOD warfighting, intelligence, and business areas of interest to be successful. To meet these goals, the J-6 must manage the entire network within the operational area and be cognizant of the performance of those portions of the GIG outside of the operational area that affect the information needs of the joint force. The three goals of NETOPS are:

(1) **Assured System and Network Availability.** Provide visibility and control over the system and network resources. Resources are effectively managed and problems are anticipated and mitigated. Proactive actions are taken to ensure the uninterrupted availability and protection of the system and network resources. This includes providing for graceful degradation, self-healing, fail over, diversity, and elimination of critical failure points.

(2) **Assured Information Protection.** Provide protection for the information passing over networks from the time it is stored and catalogued until it is distributed to the users, operators, and decisionmakers.

(3) **Assured Information Delivery.** Provide information to users, operators, and decisionmakers in a timely manner. The networks are continuously monitored to ensure the information is transferred with the correct response time, throughput, availability, and performance that meet user needs.

2. **Network Operations Responsibilities**

a. As the DOD CIO, ASD(NII) is responsible for the policy and architecture for NETOPS.

b. CJCS maintains operational oversight of the GIG through the NMCC and USSTRATCOM.

c. CDRUSSTRATCOM has the mission to direct the operation and defense of the GIG. CDRUSSTRATCOM has delegated operational and tactical level planning, force execution, and day-to-day management of the operations and defense of the GIG to USCYBERCOM.

(1) USCYBERCOM leads the operation and defense of the GIG through GIG Enterprise Management (GEM), Global Information Grid (GIG) Network Assurance (GNA), and Global Information Grid (GIG) Content Management (GCM). The JTF-GNO under USCYBERCOM, maintains SA, end-to-end management, and DOD network defense. JTF-GNO directs, manages, controls, monitors, assesses, and reports on essential elements and applications of the GIG to ensure its availability to support the needs of the President, SecDef, CCDRs, Services, agencies, business, and intelligence environments. The GNC leverages the capabilities of DISA to provide overall management, control, and technical direction of GIG and oversees a collaborative coordination process involving all CCDRs, Services, and agencies.

(2) The Services retain responsibility to provide interoperable communication systems, units, and personnel for the provision of their NETOPS requirements internal to their own theater forces and to be capable of expansion and support of other Service or multinational forces as determined by the CCDR. In addition, each Service must provide for its own NOSC and computer incident response teams according to the standards established by JTF-GNO for the IA and security of its internal networks. Services may also be tasked to operate a portion of the GIG when designated by the proper authority.

3. **Network Operations Operational Construct**

The NETOPS operational construct consists of SA, the essential tasks, and C2.

a. **Situational Awareness**

(1) A commander makes an assessment of the situation and environment by receiving information from staff elements, personal experience, reporting, other sources of information, and the COP. Once the information is collected, commanders then develop an initial understanding by putting it into a context, thus creating SA. The context is created by deducing patterns of interaction among the various factors in the operational environment. These patterns are the result of a combination of the commander's previous experience and his/her intuition. They assist the commander to arrange disparate facts into a logical and understandable construct that helps the commander to both deduce a COA and communicate complex information to others quickly and easily.

(2) JFCs operate in joint and multinational operations that encompass a multitude of units, organizations, and actors. The ability for all these players to collaborate with one another is instrumental in the success or failure of these operations. Collaboration is joint problem solving for the purpose of achieving shared understanding, making a decision, or creating a product. It allows experts to better interpret situations and problems, identify candidate actions and solutions, formulate evaluation criteria, and decide what to do. In the context of joint C2, collaboration is used to coordinate the development of decisions and actions across multiple basic C2 processes. It allows commanders to gain better SA, have a better understanding of the operational environment, better comprehend how their decisions will affect the operating

environment, and coordinate their limited resources with others. Collaboration is enabled through a collaborative information environment that allows for key collaborative C2 functions to tie together the basic C2 processes across all command levels and within all battlefield functions.

For detailed guidance on collaboration capabilities and tools employment, see CJCSM 6715.01A, Joint Collaboration Tools (CT) Employment.

(3) By sharing information, SA, and understanding, individual commanders are able to improve their ability to monitor and collect data on their environment. The individual commander is then able to develop a more thorough understanding of the situation by being able to exploit the experience and perspectives of other individual commanders. The selection of a COA and the development of plans to execute the COA can be developed and executed with the collective knowledge of the decisions and plans of others. Plan execution can be monitored by all commanders with an understanding of the assumptions and information available when the COA was developed and selected.

(4) NETOPS is an enabling capability in achieving shared SA through the GIG system, network, and information availability. GIG support to achieving SA is provided through the integrated capability to receive, correlate, and display a functional or theater-level view of systems and networks (voice, video, and data). The primary purpose is to enable a real time understanding of the impact to on-going operations as a result of degradations to the GIG and facilitate opportunities to apply immediate corrective or mitigation measures. This shared SA supported by the GIG is derived from common reporting procedures and requirements using enterprise-wide management tools within the broader issues of SA as it relates to operational impact, planning, architectures, and other factors. The GIG reporting flow is depicted in Figure IV-1. SA of the network proceeds from visibility of the intensity of activity, traffic load, and throughput potential. It enables dynamic rerouting based on priority, system status, and capacity. The effects of disruptions and intrusions are minimized through allocation of traffic to unaffected network paths. Joint and Service commanders need SA of the network to:

(a) Monitor, protect, and prioritize their networks.

(b) Assess operational impact of network disruptions.

(c) Respond to network outages/attacks.

(d) Dynamically reallocate network traffic.

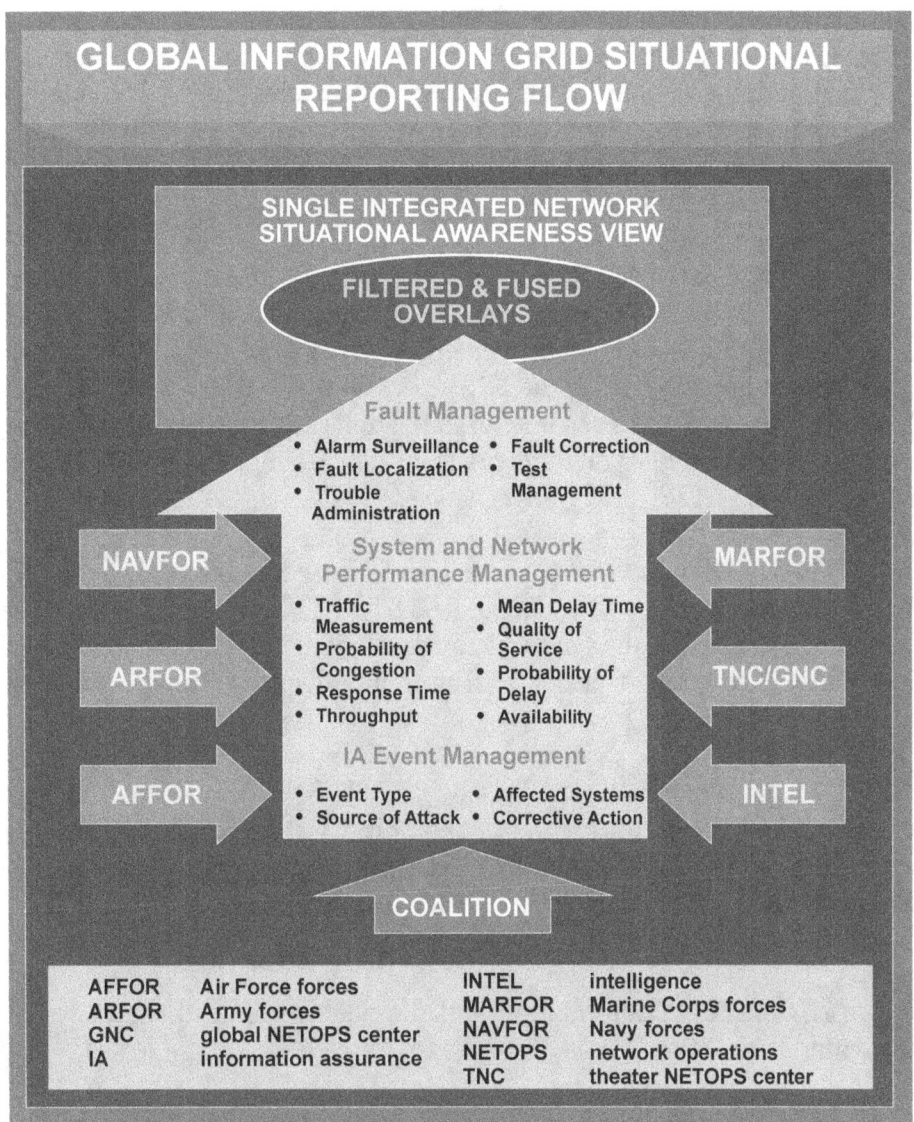

Figure IV-1. Global Information Grid Situational Reporting Flow

(5) Component, joint force, subunified command, and agency NOSCs are responsible for assimilating and integrating NETOPS SA data of their respective operational areas. Each NOSC installs, maintains, and operates network management and intrusion detection software and populates a local database to build a near real time view of their environment. Firewall configurations are maintained to ensure the integrity of the network while enabling essential GIG SA information exchange. Each local configuration database provides an input to the next echelon (e.g., base, region, theater, global). Defense-in-depth activities and installations follow the prescribed configuration so that virtual views of the entire enterprise can be created at any level.

(6) Services and agencies provide SA of their portions of the GIG to the TNCs, the GNC, JTF-GNO, USSTRATCOM, and their Service/agency leadership.

b. **Operational Construct.** The GIG operates, through cyberspace, as a globally interconnected, end-to-end, interoperable network-of-networks, which spans traditional boundaries of authority. Given the inherent global reach of the GIG, many NETOPS activities are not under the command authority of a using CCDR. Therefore, a great deal of coordination and collaboration (unity of effort) is essential to fully enable NETOPS capabilities.

(1) The JTF-GNO established the GNC through the merger of elements from the JTF Computer Network Operations' Directorate, DISA's Global NETOPS and Security Center, and the DOD computer emergency response team (CERT). In the past construct for operating and securing the DISN, the Global NETOPS and Security Center, and DOD-CERT were treated as separate organizations. DISA also established a TNC in each theater through the merger of elements from DISA's regional NETOPS and security center and the regional CERT.

(2) JTF-GNO houses the GNC and is the operational command for Global Information Grid (GIG) Network Defense (GND). The goal of the JTF-GNO is to provide support in defense of the GIG and to operationalize GND for the JFC. The JTF-GNO joint intelligence support element ensures intelligence is integrated into all JTF-GNO operations.

(3) TNCs as subordinate commands of JTF-GNO within each theater provide technical support and execution for the geographic CCDRs for those parts of the GIG under their control. The TNCs establish, maintain, and provide the theater-level portion of the GIG, extending the GIG into the theater of operations. The local SA views are provided by the supporting TNC, which will:

(a) Collect SA information and provide customized views for combatant commands within their AOR.

(b) Provide backbone connectivity and support to the GCCs in their AORs.

(4) TNCCs oversee and direct NETOPS for GCCs within their AOR to support their missions. The TNCC supports the combatant command J-6 with overall network SA sharing and coordination of NETOPS activities throughout the GIG. The primary mission of the TNCC is to lead, prioritize, and direct resources to ensure they are optimized to support the geographic GCCs' assigned missions and operations, and to advise the GCCs of the ability of the GIG to support current and future operations. The specific roles of the TNCC include:

(a) Monitoring of the theater portion of the GIG.

(b) Determining operational impact of major degradations and outages.

(c) Coordinating responses to degradations and outages that affect joint operations.

(d) Coordinating GIG actions in support of changing operational priorities.

(5) Global Network Operations (NETOPS) control centers (GNCCs) oversee and coordinate NETOPS for functional CCDRs to support their missions. The GNCC supports the combatant command J-6 with overall network SA sharing and performs coordination of NETOPS activities throughout the GIG. Functional combatant commands will establish a GNCC to oversee and coordinate NETOPS to support their missions. Functional CCDRs will exercise OPCON of their portions of the GIG through their GNCC. The GNCC will establish operational priorities for and impact assessments of NETOPS actions in support of their missions. The GNC and TNCs will provide general support to the GNCCs.

(6) NOSCs, established by a Service and agency resource owner, coordinate their NETOPS activities with the GNC, TNCC, or GNCC and other NETOPS centers as appropriate. An NOSC acts for the Service or agency to ensure all required GIG SA data is collected and shared, that network components comply with DOD and joint directives, and the GIG COP is maintained for SA.

(7) The JNCC manages the tactical communications of the joint force, serving as the NOSC for the deployed portion of the GIG supporting a joint force. It exercises staff supervision over network service centers belonging to deployed components and subordinate commands. The JNCC provides the appropriate TNCC with:

(a) Local SA information (directly to TNCC and TNC).

(b) Mission impact assessments of system and network events.

(c) GIG requirements beyond the JFC's current assets or authority.

(8) The Commander, JTF-GNO created the Global Network Operations (NETOPS) Support Center (GNSC) as a subordinate command to provide the day-to-day technical operation, control, and management of the portions of the GIG that support global operations but are not assigned to a combatant command. This organization was created from the DISA CONUS Regional NETOPS and Security Center. The GNSC conducts GIG backbone NETOPS, DOD Gateway mission support, provisioning of provided services, network engineering, circuit implementation, and intertheater connectivity from CONUS to the Pacific, European, Southern, and Southwest Asian theaters. The GNSC provides general support to the GCCs and TNCs. The GNSC provides direct support to the functional CCDRs. Functional CCDRs have a global mission, often providing support to the GCCs, and have a global requirement for NETOPS support. Some functional combatant commands operate their own global networks. As such, the functional CCDRs receive direct support from the GNSC and general support from USSTRATCOM, JTF-GNO, and all TNCs. Functional CCDRs exercise OPCON over their portions of the GIG through their GNCC. The GNCC coordinates the functional CCDR's NETOPS requirements with the GNSC and the TNCCs.

(9) Effective GND operations require a partnership of NETOPS, law enforcement, intelligence, and command leadership. The National Coordinating Center (NCC) of the NCS is another member of the global NETOPS team. The NCC runs an Information Sharing and Analysis Center, a joint industry/government center that coordinates initiation and restoration of telecommunications services during national emergencies.

(10) A NETOPS event is a collective term for all NETOPS activities that have the potential to significantly and negatively impact the operational readiness of the GIG. To effectively operate the GIG globally while realizing the GCCs' requirements to direct GIG operations in their theaters, an event-based C2 structure is used for GIG operations. C2 of GIG operations will be based on the situation at the time. The three possible circumstances that determine the C2 of NETOPS are known as global, theater, and non-global NETOPS events.

(a) Global NETOPS events are those activities that have the potential to impact the operational readiness of the GIG and require a coordinated response. CDRUSSTRATCOM is the supported commander for global NETOPS events and will issue orders and direction through JTF-GNO.

(b) Theater NETOPS events are those activities occurring within a theater that have the potential to impact the operations in that theater. The affected GCC is the supported command for theater NETOPS events. USSTRATCOM is a supporting command to the affected GCC for theater NETOPS events.

(c) Non-global NETOPS events are those activities whose impact affects functional CCDRs, unassigned Title 10, USC, forces, or DOD agencies and are neither global nor theater in nature. CDRUSSTRATCOM is the supported commander for non-global NETOPS events.

c. Joint NETOPS is an integrated approach to GEM, GNA, and GCM.

(1) **GIG Enterprise Management.** GEM is defined as the technology, processes, and policy necessary to effectively operate the systems and networks that comprise the GIG. This essential task merges IT services with the NETOPS critical capabilities.

(2) **GIG Network Assurance.** GNA incorporates protection, detection, and response of any unauthorized activities against the GIG. It provides end-to-end protection to ensure data quality and protection against unauthorized access and inadvertent damage or modification. GNA incorporates IA protection activities, CND, and critical information protection. This is not intended to replace the terms of IA and CND. Additionally, GIG constituent systems that meet the definition of a national security system (NSS) must follow the appropriate IA guidelines and policies for NSS.

Other GIG systems not designated NSS must be provided adequate IA so as not to jeopardize the security of GIG NSS.

(3) **GIG Content Management.** GCM provides awareness of relevant, accurate information through automated access to newly discovered or recurring information in a timely, efficient, and usable format.

(4) **Defense-in-Depth**

(a) DOD relies on digital electronic information capabilities to store, process, and move essential information to plan, direct, coordinate, and execute operations. Cyberspace threats are a real and imminent danger to the GIG. These sophisticated threats can exploit security weaknesses. Robust IA and securing vital networks and data is a high priority. The current cyberspace defense strategy is to reduce vulnerabilities and mitigate the threat by linking our nation's offensive and defensive capabilities. Weaknesses that can be exploited become vulnerabilities that can jeopardize the most sensitive components of information capabilities. However, we can employ deep, layered defenses to reduce vulnerabilities and recover after an attack.

(b) GND requires a defense-in-depth strategy that integrates the capabilities of people, technology, and operations to establish multi-layer and multidimensional protection to ensure survivability and mission accomplishment. GND is important to the JFC's ability to conduct warfare and other military operations. A shared-risk environment is created when a vulnerable system connects to other systems that trust it to be secure; it, thereby, exposes the other systems to exploitation by adversaries. Defense-in-depth must ensure that the level of protection of one system is not undermined by vulnerabilities of other interconnected systems. The underlying principles of this strategy are applicable to any information system or network, regardless of organization. Figure IV-2 illustrates the principal aspects of the defense-in-depth strategy.

(c) To counter different attack methods, the JFC must employ a variety of security methods. The weaknesses of one safeguard mechanism should be protected by the strengths of another. To block threats to different locations in the protected environment, the JFC must deploy defenses at multiple locations or layers. In principal, no sector or avenue of approach into the sensitive environment of the information system should be unprotected. The security measures may not be uniform but must be interoperable, coexisting in the same environment. They cannot impose unacceptable computing, communications, or organizational burdens and obstacles that hamper accomplishment of vital operations. They should work together in such functions as sharing data and providing cues, indications, or triggers to perform actions.

1. People

a. People use technologies to conduct GND practices and are the central element of defense-in-depth. Information systems and the information they

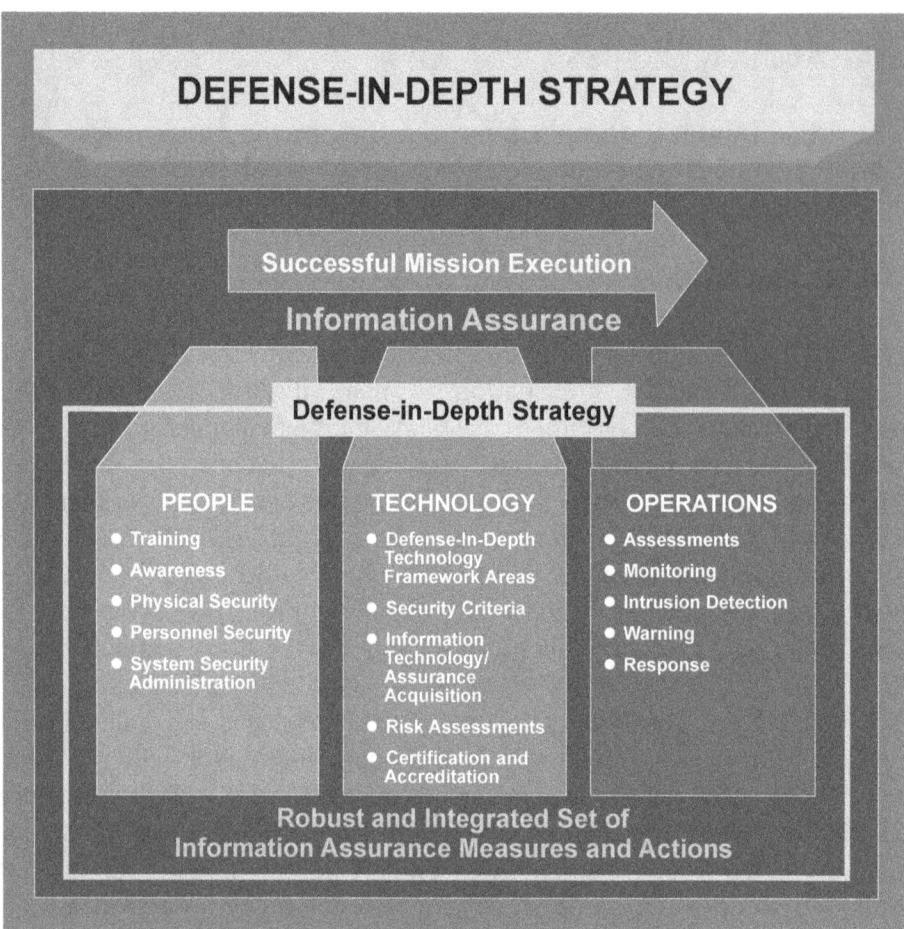

Figure IV-2. Defense-in-Depth Strategy

process need protection from unauthorized actions that jeopardize their ability to function effectively.

b. The JFC is responsible for protection of information and the communications system. The trained and aware user is the first and most vital line of defense. A comprehensive program of education, training, practical experience, and awareness should be provided to the members of the joint force and mission partners. The defense of DOD networks must be accountable to the highest levels, and managed as such. It is imperative that commanders enforce measures to ensure the readiness of networks managed by personnel under their purview. Discipline and diligence will help prevent our adversaries from exploiting and successfully attacking our networks.

c. Every person who creates, uses, manages, destroys, oversees, or administers information systems (military, government civilian, contractor, and foreign national) has a responsible security role. Key roles include the system administrator, IA manager, IA officer, and DAA.

2. Technology. A collection of local computing devices interconnected via LAN, governed by a single security policy, regardless of physical location is considered an "enclave." The enclave boundary is the point at which information enters or leaves the enclave or organization. The JFC must protect the vital lines of electronic communication that link the local computing environment enclaves. Some important technologies that help defend these networks include:

a. Redundant and multiple data paths.

b. Automated tools for monitoring and management.

c. Intrusion detection.

d. Firewalls and guards.

e. Malicious code and virus detectors.

f. Biometrics.

g. Cryptography and encryption.

h. Protected distribution systems.

3. Operations

a. Defense-in-depth requires widely distributed intrusion detection activities to recognize and describe activities that are different from the normal pattern or fit known "bad" patterns, and to limit and contain the access across networks that a malicious user may exploit. The nature and scope of the incident, effects, cause, and vulnerability must be determined. After an intrusion is detected, incident information must be reported through established channels to appropriate authorities, specialized analysis, and response centers. Incident response begins with immediate local emergency damage-limitation and survivability actions that should be stated in organizational information systems security policy, procedures, tactics, and training guidance (e.g., standard operating procedures, contingency plans, and others) and implemented promptly.

b. **INFOCON.** The INFOCON system provides a framework within which the CDRUSSTRATCOM, GCCs, Service chiefs, base/post/camp/station/ vessel commanders, and agency heads can measure and report the readiness of their networks to match operational priorities. The framework is a set of prescribed and optional actions and cycles necessary for reestablishing the confidence level and security of information systems for the commander. INFOCON operates within an environment of "defense-in-depth" and supports that strategy by returning critical assets to a secure baseline at a specified operating tempo. GCCs have the authority to change INFOCONs within their AORs. Functional CCDRs have the authority to change INFOCONs for the unique systems and networks supporting their mission areas. Local (base/post/camp/station/vessel) commanders have the authority to change INFOCONs for their information systems and networks. The system provides a predefined sequence of actions necessary for achieving a common level of INFOSEC for DOD information systems. The INFOCON system is characterized by predefined directive defensive postures designed to mitigate risk. The information assurance vulnerability management (IAVM) program is the comprehensive distribution process to notify CCDRs, Services, and agencies about vulnerabilities and the corresponding corrective actions.

c. CND response actions, tailored response options, and thorough analysis of events across the information systems provide for strengthening of the JFC's defensive posture, eliminating or reducing attack effects, and focusing response efforts to threats to the JFC information and information system.

For additional information on the INFOCON system and the IAVM program, see CJCSM 6510.01, Defense-In-Depth: Information Assurance (IA) and Computer Network Defense (CND).

(d) The use of EW tactics such as spectrum jamming needs to be taken into account both for how it affects enemies as well as its potential to unavoidably disrupt joint/coalition communications.

5. **Management of the Global Information Grid**

a. **USSTRATCOM has overall responsibility for global NETOPS and defense in coordination with CJCS and the other combatant commands.**

b. **GIG Configuration Management**

(1) Uniform configuration management of the GIG ensures interoperability and survivability of the DOD IA. In addition to the expected adherence to DOD policy, **GIG configuration is controlled through compliance with the GIG architecture.** GIG assets, to include those that are commercial off-the-shelf, are to be configured IAW approved information assurance policy, capabilities, documents, and standards and be compliant with the operational, system, and technical views of the GIG architecture.

(2) Operational assets are also uniformly configured to ensure architecture standards compliance, INFOSEC, operational effectiveness, and efficiency and quality of service across the GIG. **Configuration control boards (CCBs)** are often used to determine and regulate actual communications system configurations. The **theater joint tactical networks (TJTNs) CCB** is one such board that, as its charter states, seeks to coordinate initiatives, control the configuration of systems and networks, and synchronize the acquisition and fielding of the software and hardware products associated with the deployed networks of the GIG. **The Army is the Executive Agent for TJTN.** Together with the TJTN CCB, the Army oversees and coordinates development and life-cycle enhancement of theater-deployable networked communications system to achieve DOD

compatibility, interoperability, and integration objectives for systems composing the TJTN. ASD(NII) participates in an advisory capacity (see Figure IV-3).

(3) GIG assets of the combatant commands, Services, and agencies are configured generally to meet the requirements of the command being served; however, **the priority requirement is to support the NMCS** (see Chapter V, "Communications System Support to the President, the Secretary of Defense, and the Intelligence Community" for further details on the NMCS). GIG assets of a combatant command also include the GIG assets of subordinate unified commands and JTFs when such organizations are established and assigned or attached.

c. The **DOD CIO (ASD[NII])** is responsible for developing, maintaining, and enforcing compliance with the GIG architecture. Inherent in the CIO's architecture responsibility is to enforce interoperability, IA, net-centric data sharing, use of services, and program synchronization.

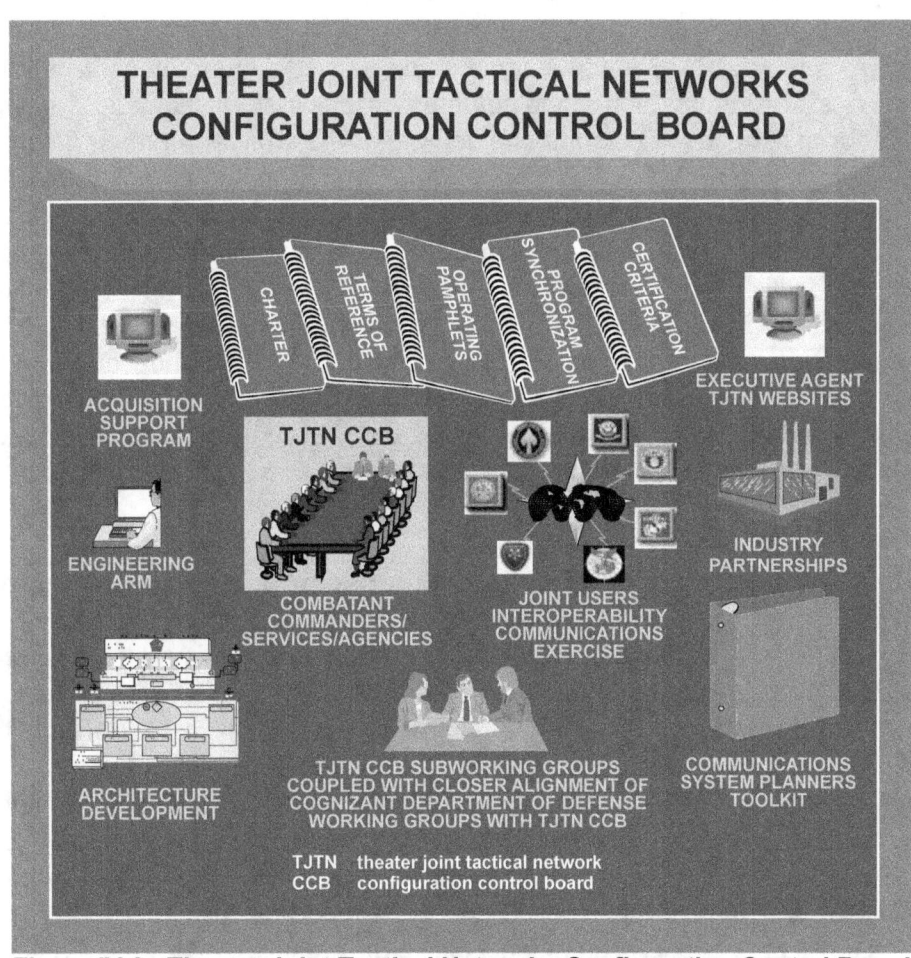

Figure IV-3. Theater Joint Tactical Networks Configuration Control Board

d. The GIG is essentially a global network that combines the specific communications system capabilities of the DOD components. Operation and defense of the GIG is largely a matter of overarching common processes, standards, and protocols orchestrated by USSTRATCOM. The purposes of this framework are to govern common activities by all subscribers, deal with competing demands for service, and solicit essential joint force support from relevant agencies. CJCS, DISA, and the Services ensure that commanders at each echelon have the necessary capabilities to employ the GIG to accomplish their assigned missions. CJCS is responsible for operational network policy and overall direction of the DISN as DOD's primary and global provider of GIG joint information services and information systems. This oversight responsibility does not infer command authority and is executed and facilitated through the assistance of the NMCC, as well as through USSTRATCOM's global NETOPS C2 structure. Non-DOD IC agencies retain C2 of their respective networks and assets which interface with the GIG in support of warfighting and other national interests. They interface at the SCI level via JWICS, in compliance with the guidance and directions of the Director, Central Intelligence Agency. The GIG networks are controlled within a tiered management hierarchy consisting of global, regional, and local control centers enabling a survivable, flexible, and disciplined C2 capability for DOD's GIG.

e. **DISA has established TNCs** to provide a single point of contact for theater network services, operations status, and communications system anomalies. Each TNC is responsible for the effective operation and defense of the GIG within their theater and for providing support to the GCC. The TNC develops, monitors, and maintains a GIG SA view for the theater and provides that SA to the GCC and JTF-GNO. These control centers also serve as a central point of contact for operational matters in support of a GCC. In some theaters, CCDRs have established a TNCC or equivalent organization, as an adjunct to the JOC, to gain network SA, as well as to assess operational impact when network anomalies arise. These organizations interface with component control centers within the theater. At the joint force level, the J-6 establishes a JNCC to manage and control joint networks. This is another local control center in the GIG operational hierarchy. As such, it also interfaces with Service component control centers in the operational area.

f. Regardless of the source, **GIG resources assigned to CCDRs operate under their COCOM** and are an integral part of their C2 system until such time as the President, SecDef, or the CCDRs determine that further support is no longer needed or a higher priority necessitates redeployment of the assets. The command authority and responsibilities of the GCCs include control, review, and coordination of assigned GIG resources and actions affecting such resources within the GCC's AOR. CCDRs coordinate and direct NETOPS activities consistent with USSTRATCOM guidance to ensure the availability and protection of the GIG. GCCs have the authority to change INFOCONs within their AORs. Functional CCDRs have the authority to change INFOCONs for the unique systems and networks supporting their mission areas. Local (base/post/camp/station/vessel) commanders have the authority to change INFOCONs for their information systems and networks. Local commanders may only raise INFOCON above applicable baseline, unless granted waiver by controlling INFOCON authority.

g. CCDRs normally develop plans that integrate the DISN, NCS, commercial, and multinational systems as well as organize joint and Service organic and component tactical GIG assets into interoperable and compatible theater networks to support their mission. As a part of their planning, CCDRs determine priorities for information flow and allocate network resources, to include bandwidth within the AOR of their commands, and those required by component and other subordinate commands. **The GCCs exercise oversight over their theater portion of the GIG through their support relationship with DISA regional offices, as well as through those forces assigned to them in the Forces for Unified Commands Memorandum, or as modified by deployment orders.**

h. Operating elements of the DISN are subject to authoritative direction from different sources because of ownership. However, IAW DODD 5105.19, *Defense Information Systems Agency (DISA)*, **DISA field organizations, under the command of the Director, DISA, exercise operational direction (the authoritative direction necessary to ensure the effective operation of the DISN) over the DISN operating elements.** Directors of DISA field organizations as well as Service component commanders though, will be responsive to the operational needs of the CCDRs, who exercise COCOM over the Service component operating elements of the DISN. GCCs develop agreements that clearly delineate the commanders' relationships with the DISA field organizations within their AORs. In exercising COCOM, the CCDRs are cognizant of DISN support to the President and SecDef, DOD agencies, and other CCDRs, and preserve DISN integrity and standards to the maximum possible extent. With respect to the DISN, DISA coordinates and controls the provisioning of network services across the DISN transport network and across service delivery points or demarcation lines (which are associated with the ownership and subsequent technical control of GIG resources), IAW CCDR requirements. CCDR planners must acknowledge the highly integrated nature of their theater network as a part of the GIG. Consequently, development of communications system annexes to their campaign plans and OPLANs requires close coordination among their components to include DISA field operating commands, to ensure interoperability among forces.

Intentionally Blank

CHAPTER V
COMMUNICATIONS SYSTEM SUPPORT TO THE PRESIDENT, THE SECRETARY OF DEFENSE, AND THE INTELLIGENCE COMMUNITY

> *"It is recognized that the President's responsibilities as Head of Government complicate the problem of ensuring his survivability as Commander-in-Chief. This latter survivability is achieved by providing for survivability of the Office as distinct from survivability of the man."*
>
> **National Military Communications System Master Plan**

1. National Military Command System

a. The NMCS is the priority component of the GIG designed to support the President, SecDef, and the JCS in the exercise of their responsibilities. The NMCS provides the means by which the President and SecDef can receive warning and intelligence so that accurate and timely decisions can be made, the resources of the Services can be applied, military missions can be assigned, and direction can be communicated to CCDRs or the commanders of other commands. Both the communication of warning and intelligence from all sources and the communication of decisions and commands to military forces require that the NMCS be a responsive, reliable, and survivable system. An enduring command structure with survivable GIG systems is both required and fundamental to NMCS continuity of operations.

b. The NMCS command nodes are the NMCC, the National Airborne Operations Center, the USSTRATCOM Global Operations Center (for essential emergency actions only), USSTRATCOM distributed C2 nodes, and the United States Northern Command Mobile Consolidated Command Center, and other command centers as designated by SecDef. Support of the NMCS is the priority function of all primary and alternate command centers. These centers are continuously staffed and ready for use, linked by reliable GIG infrastructure and supported by warning and intelligence systems. Special capabilities within the GIG provide for communication with strategic offensive and defensive forces and for other forces that may be required for quick reaction in crises. In this case, the communications will be designated and operated to ensure minimum elapsed time for the transmission of orders to the operating units of these forces. The NMCS also includes infrastructure connecting NMCS centers with primary and alternate command centers of the following:

    (1) HQ of the combatant commands.

    (2) HQ of the Services.

    (3) Other designated commands and DOD agencies that provide support through the GCCS family of systems.

    (4) Major or key intelligence direction, analysis, and indication and warning centers.

(5) Other functional activities (e.g., counterdrug).

c. The GIG also supports effective coordination and liaison with those activities of the US Government outside DOD that have functions associated with the NMCS (e.g., the White House Situation Room, Department of State Operations Center, Department of Homeland Security, Federal Bureau of Investigation, and Federal Emergency Management Agency. Central Intelligence Agency Operations Center, the National Coordinating Center for Telecommunications, United Nations Military Mission, United States Coast Guard Command Center, Federal Aviation Administration Executive Communications Control Center), and other agencies, activities, or centers as designated. The GIG supports homeland defense and civil support (to include defense support of civil authorities) by enabling DOD and the interagency mission partners to seamlessly share vital information. Military information flows to these command and operations elements through the NMCS, using GIG communications systems. In addition, political, intelligence, diplomatic, and economic information for the NMCS is provided by these same systems. Finally, the NMCS provides communications to support representatives of the White House and other government activities that may use the NMCS in a politico-military situation concerning strategic direction of US military forces.

d. The GIG provides for lateral coordination with US Government activities external to DOD for interchange of data to and from the NMCS.

2. Nuclear Command and Control

General operational responsibility for the Nuclear Command and Control System (NCCS) lies with CJCS and is centrally directed through the Joint Staff. The NCCS supports the Presidential nuclear C2 of the combatant commands in the areas of integrated tactical warning and attack assessment, decisionmaking, decision dissemination, and force management and report back. To accomplish this, the NCCS comprises those critical communications system components of the GIG that provide connectivity from the President and SecDef through the NMCS to the CCDRs with nuclear capabilities and nuclear execution forces. It includes the emergency action message dissemination systems and those systems used for tactical warning/attack assessment, conferencing, force report back, reconnaissance, retargeting, force management, and requests for permission to use nuclear weapons. The NCCS is integral to and ensures performance of critical strategic functions of the GCCS family and systems. The Minimum Essential Emergency Communications Network provides assured communications connectivity between the President and the strategic deterrent forces in stressed environments.

3. Intelligence Community

a. The joint intelligence systems architecture is an integral part of the GIG. Although intelligence organizations use a variety of sensors and other information sources to collect and analyze data and produce intelligence products, the communications system support to intelligence is normally limited to providing the communications interface and media required to move intelligence and related information. Communications system support does not typically cover the collection and production of intelligence.

b. DODIIS

(1) DODIIS is the combination of personnel, procedures, equipment, computer programs, and supporting communications that support the timely and comprehensive preparation and presentation of intelligence information to military commanders and national-level decisionmakers. DIA is responsible for implementing and managing the configuration of information, data, and communications standards for DOD intelligence systems and for IC systems that interface with, or directly support DOD. As such, DIA establishes defense-wide intelligence priorities for attaining interoperability between the tactical, theater, and national intelligence systems and the respective communications system at each level.

(2) In a technical sense, DODIIS is the SCI portion of the GIG that provides the interface between the CCDRs and the IC. The joint intelligence systems architecture is an integral part of the GIG, and consists of an integrated network supporting voice, data, and VTC. The JWICS, the Joint Deployable Intelligence Support System, and the Distributed Common Ground System currently form the foundation of the SCI portion of the GIG. This interface consists of more than the SCI networks. DODIIS also provides the interfaces between the JWICS SCI IC systems and the SIPRNET IC systems. It is through this interface that much of the real time intelligence gathered by the CCDRs is passed up into the national IC systems and the national intelligence products are passed back down to the CCDRs. Additionally, this interface extends multinational networks that are essential partners in today's missions. As such, DODIIS has evolved into an enterprise consisting of mission applications, communications services, and user equipment consolidated under centralized management to better serve the CCDRs and provide more responsive intelligence. This consolidation is shaped around an enterprise approach using regional service centers (RSCs). The globally linked RSCs provide the foundation and interface for data to be managed as a single enterprise entity transparent to the users. Data will reside on, or be accessible through the enterprise that connects the policy makers, analysts, planners, and decisionmakers in support of the joint force.

4. National Communications System

a. The NCS, consisting of federal member departments and agencies, is responsible for ensuring the availability of a viable national security emergency preparedness (NSEP) telecommunications infrastructure (see Figure V-1). The NCS consists of the telecommunications assets of the entities represented on the NCS Committee of Principals and an administrative structure consisting of the executive agent, the NCS Committee of Principals, and the manager. The NCS includes, to the extent permitted by law, other executive entities that bear policy, regulatory, or enforcement responsibilities of importance to NSEP telecommunications capabilities. The assets are operated and funded by their respective parent agencies, pursuant to cross-Service or mutual support arrangements. The Department of Homeland Security's Undersecretary for Information Assurance and Infrastructure Protection manages the NCS.

b. The addition of competitive service providers with multiple points of contact within industry for planning and service provisioning has complicated the means for satisfying NSEP telecommunications requirements. To help manage how service providers are selected, the National Security Telecommunications Advisory Committee (NSTAC) was established in 1982 by Executive Order 12382, President's NSTAC. Composed of chief executives from major telecommunications and IT-related companies, the NSTAC provides the President with a unified source of national security telecommunications policy expertise unobtainable solely within the Federal Government. While the NCS Committee of Principals serves as the mechanism for federal interagency coordination, the NSTAC and its working group structure are the means for the NCS to work with industry to address the range of NSEP telecommunications issues. The Joint Staff J-6 engages with the NCS through participation on the NSTAC.

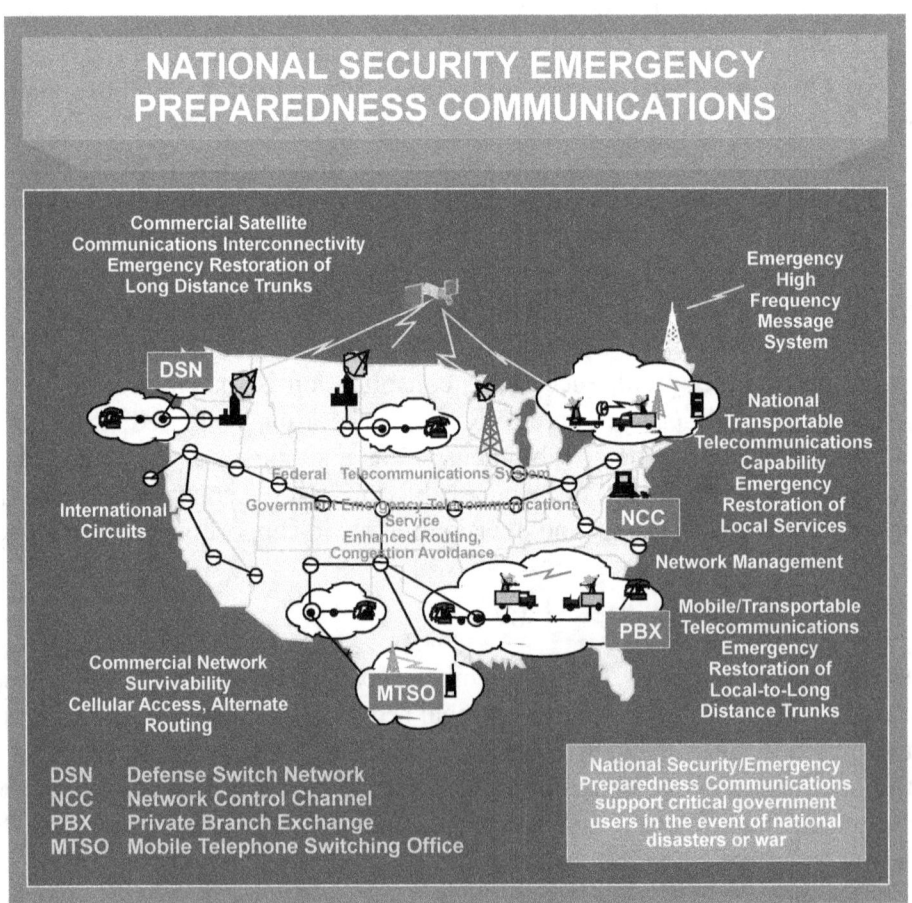

Figure V-1. National Security Emergency Preparedness Communications

APPENDIX A
GLOBAL INFORMATION GRID COMPONENTS

1. The Seven Global Information Grid Components

The seven GIG components are: warrior, global applications, computing, communications, NETOPS, information management, and foundation (see Figure A-1).

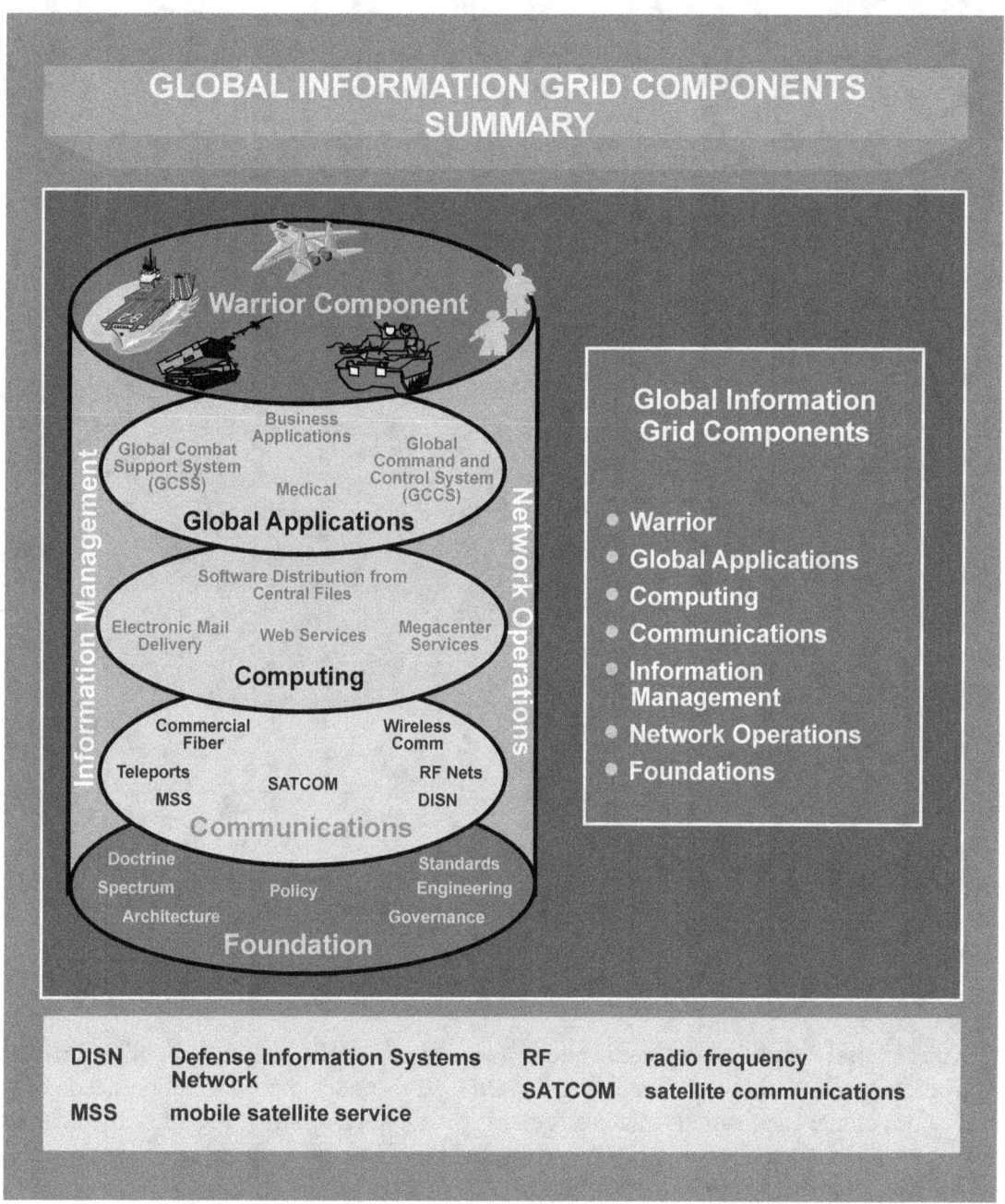

Figure A-1. Global Information Grid Components Summary

2. Warrior Component

The joint force is directly connected to the network by the GIG **warrior component.** The warrior component is the personal, shipboard, track-, vehicle-, and aircraft-mounted radios, computers, software, and display devices that directly contribute to SA, collaboration, and access to information critical to combat operations to the decisionmaker/shooter (see Figure A-2). All components of the GIG support the warrior component.

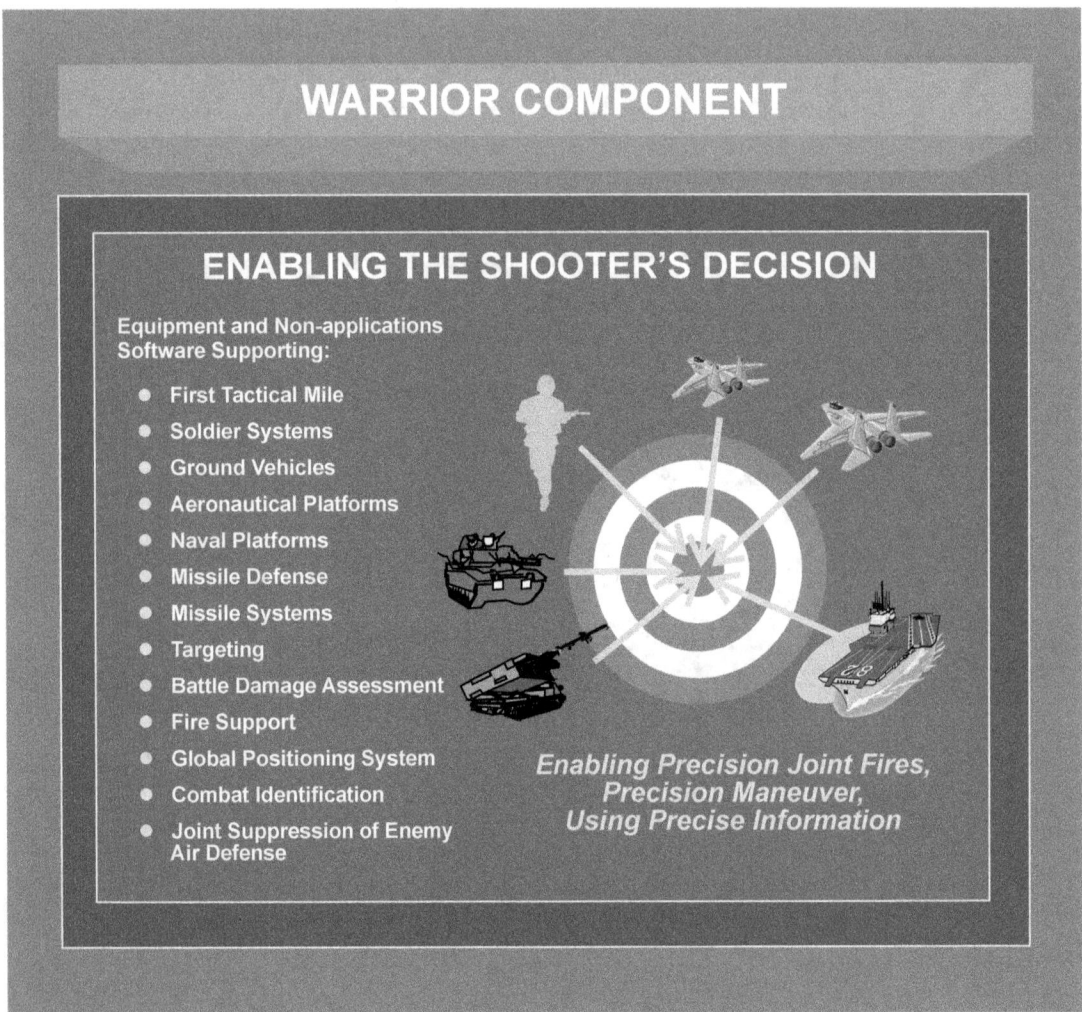

Figure A-2. Warrior Component

3. Global Applications Component

The **global applications component** (see Figure A-3) is the set of information applications used by the joint force over the GIG. It provides the information needs of the force and includes applications in areas such as fire support, weather, logistics, medical, and business. The GCCS-J, the GCSS-J, and the AMHS are three critical applications of the thousands supporting DOD.

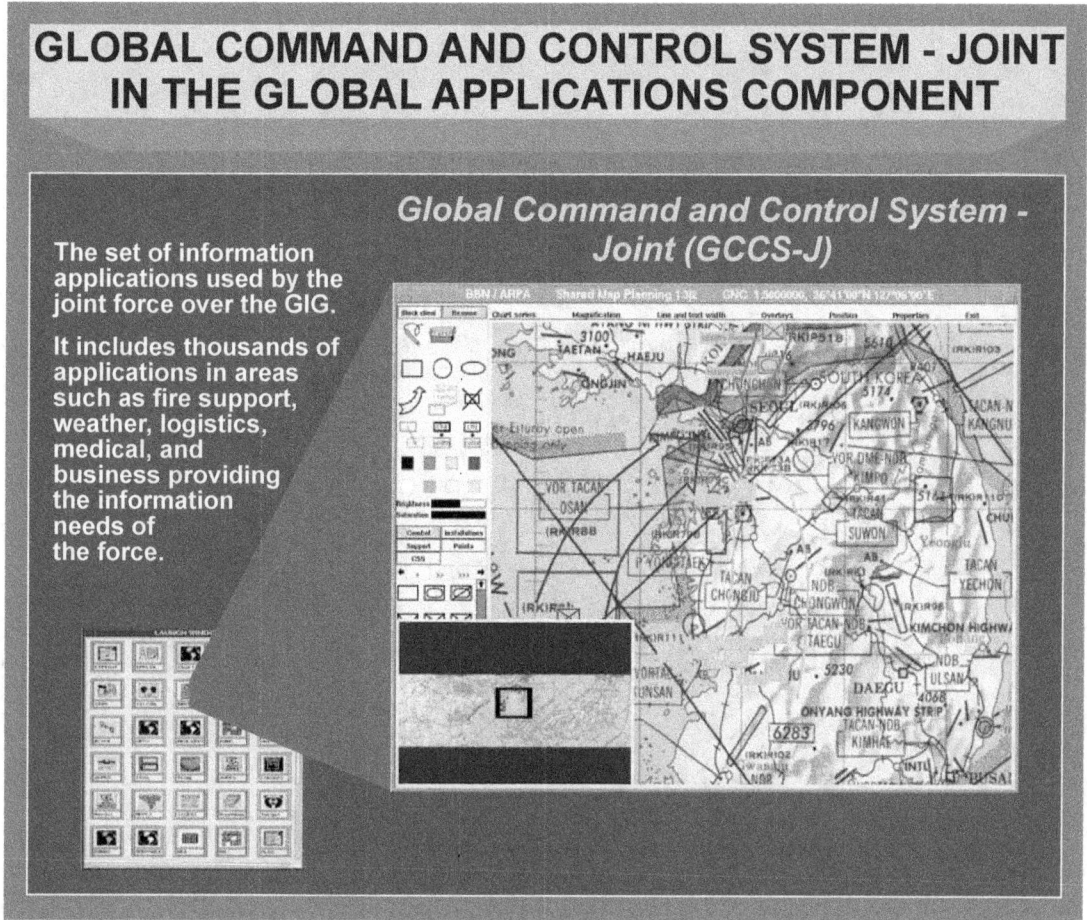

Figure A-3. Global Command and Control System – Joint in the Global Applications Component

4. **Computing Component**

The **computing component** (Figure A-4) consists of hardware, software, and processes. It includes search services, shared data warehouses for storage/access, software distribution from central locations, shared mapping services, licensing services, electronic mail delivery, web services, common directories, and collaboration services to share information and ideas. The DISA defense enterprise computing centers can provide a significant portion of these services to the joint force.

5. **Communications Component**

The **communications component** (Figure A-5) provides common-user information transport and processing services to all DOD users. It extends from the local base post, camp, station, and ship through the strategic networks, to the user. To achieve this, Service FMOs work directly with combatant command FMOs to coordinate and negotiate the electromagnetic spectrum supportability of the communications components (e.g., electromagnetic spectrum dependent devices). The communications component includes a mixture of DOD and commercial communications including global fiber, the aerial layer, SATCOM, wireless, radio frequency nets, and ever evolving, more capable DOD

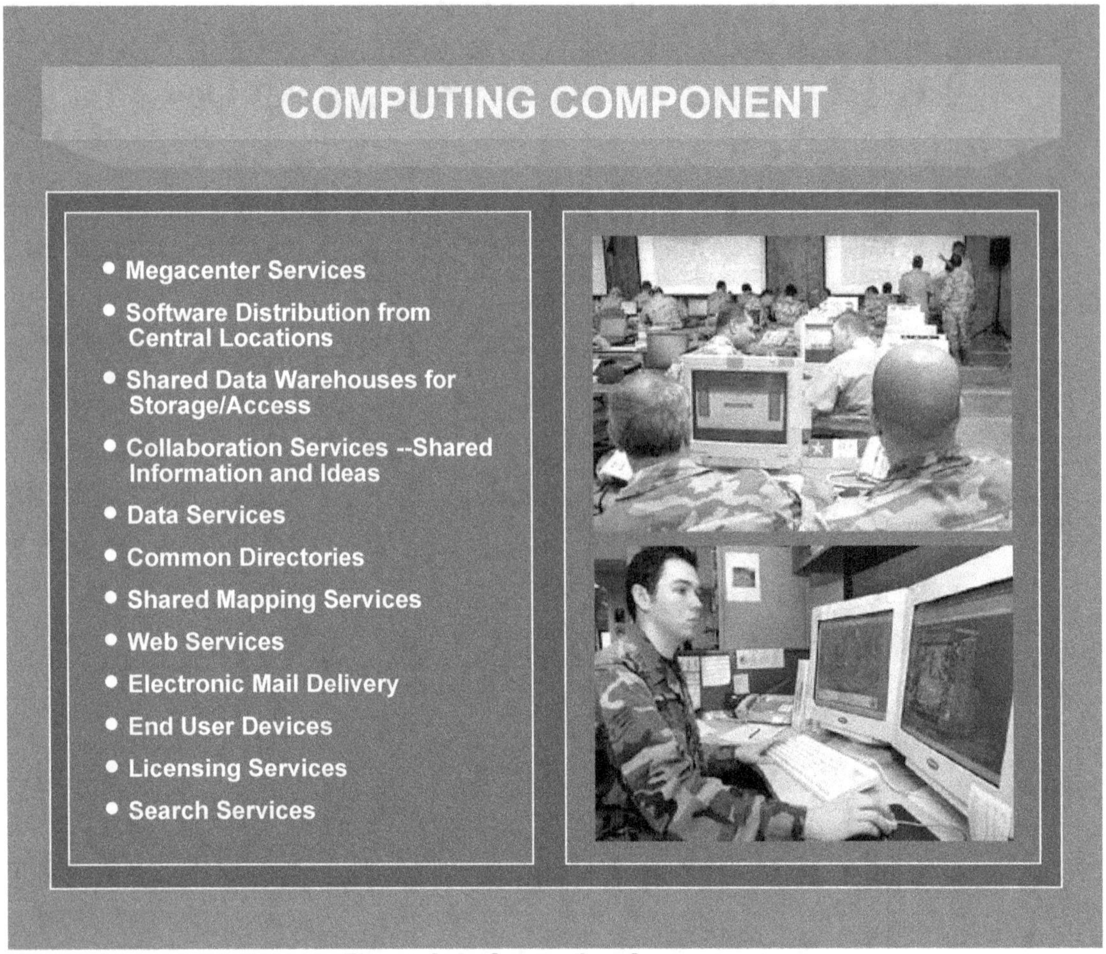

Figure A-4. Computing Component

Gateway sites. DOD Gateway sites connect the joint force to the DISN long-haul services to provide a reachback capability for DISN voice, data, and video services across all frequency bands. The DISN provides the joint force with the ability to access needed capabilities worldwide.

6. **Network Operations Component**

a. NETOPS provides integrated end-to-end management of networks, global applications, and services across the GIG to provide network visibility to enabling commanders to manage their networks as they would other battle systems. The GNC command center provides worldwide network monitoring, contingency support, network crisis action support, network resolution management, and network IA integration. USSTRATCOM executes DOD global network operations through USCYBERCOM.

b. NETOPS provides integrated network visibility and end-to-end management of networks, global applications, and services across the GIG and facilitates net-centric operations. It provides the service assurance goals of: **assured system and network availability, assured information protection, and assured information delivery.**

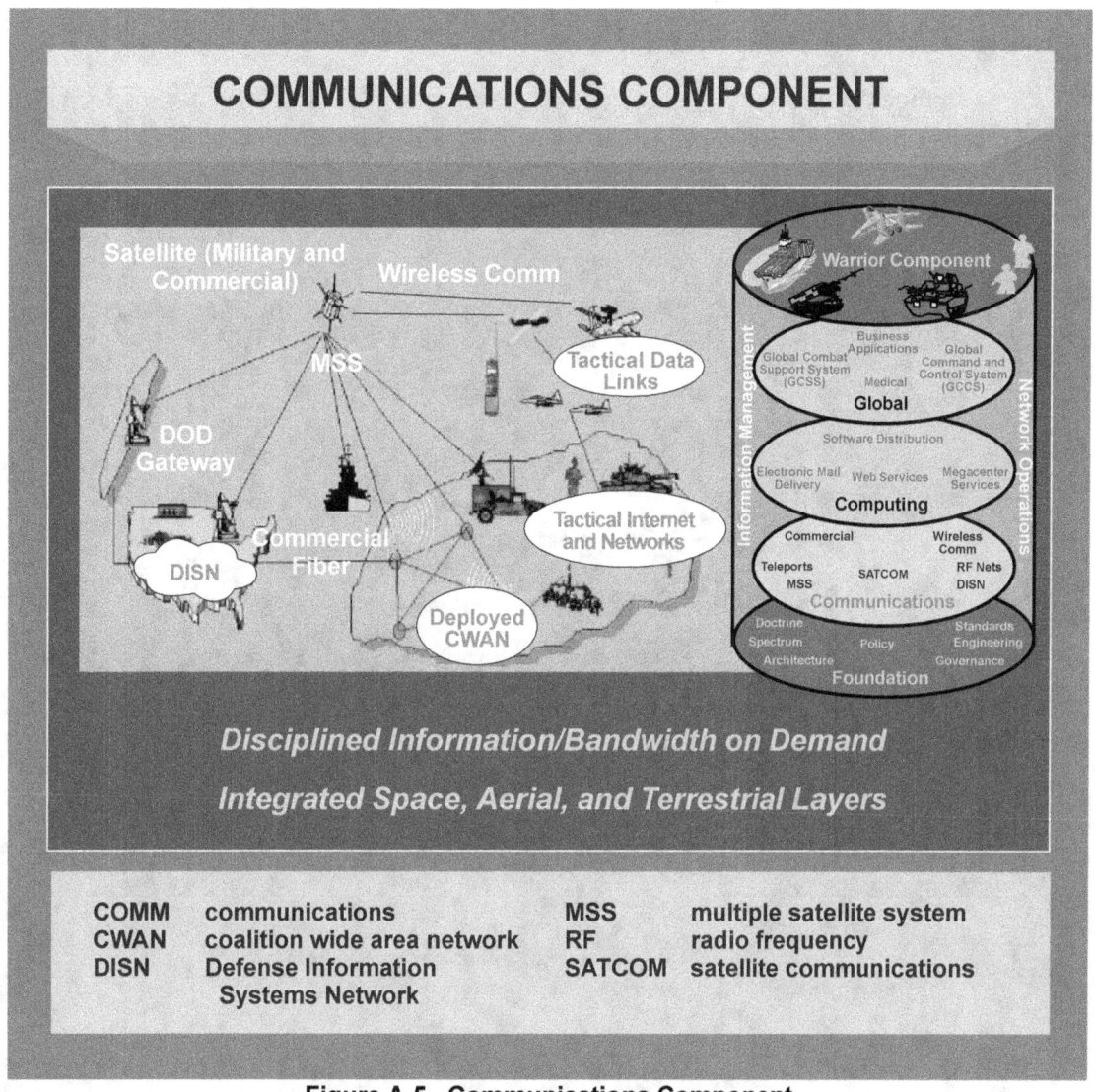

Figure A-5. Communications Component

There are three significant attributes of NETOPS: **SA, the operational construct, and mission essential tasks.**

c. **SA** is an enabling capability of NETOPS. GIG SA is the integrated capability to receive, correlate, and display a functional or theater-level view of systems and networks (voice, video, and data). The primary purpose is to enhance knowledge of the GIG to collaboratively improve the quality and speed of decisionmaking regarding the employment, protection, and defense of the GIG.

d. Given the inherent global reach of the GIG, many global NETOPS activities are not under the command authority of a using CCDR. Therefore, a great deal of coordination and collaboration (unity of effort) is essential in the **operational construct** of NETOPS to fully enable NETOPS capabilities.

e. As depicted in Figure A-6 the **essential tasks** of GIG NETOPS are GEM, GNA, and GCM.

NETOPS and its subcomponents are discussed in Chapter IV, "Network Operations."

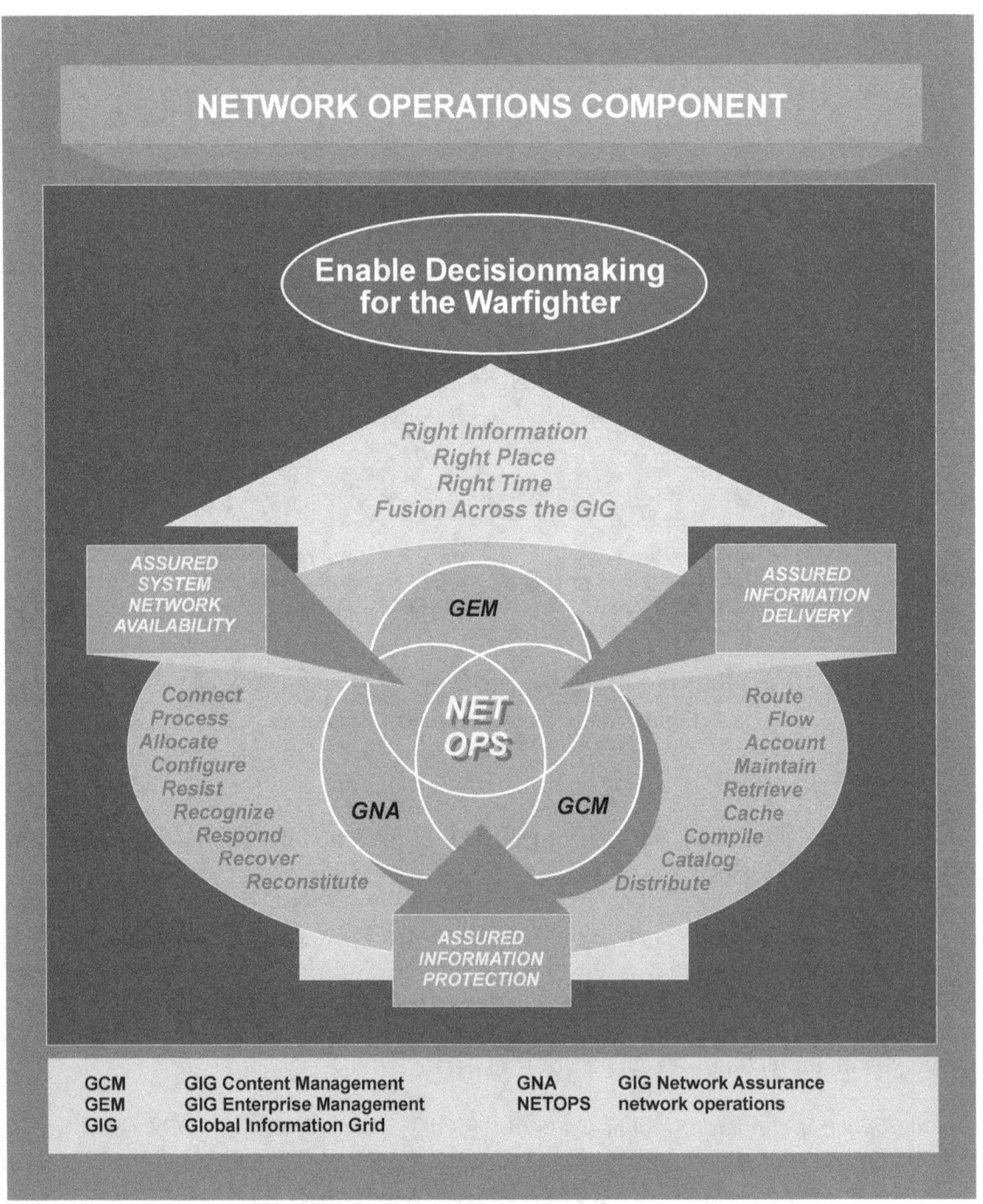

Figure A-6. Network Operations Component

7. Information Management Component

The **IM component** enables the planning, manipulating, and controlling of information throughout its life cycle (e.g., creation or collection, processing, dissemination, use, storage, and disposition). The IM component allows the joint force to access needed databases with appropriate permissions, anywhere in the world. IM provides joint forces with the critical ability to dynamically tailor and prioritize their information requirements to support the mission and environment. IDM discussed earlier as a subset of NETOPS is also a subset of IM. While some boundaries have been established, this does not mean IDM is totally divorced from the production of information or the presentation of information. Figure A-7 depicts the IM/IDM relationship.

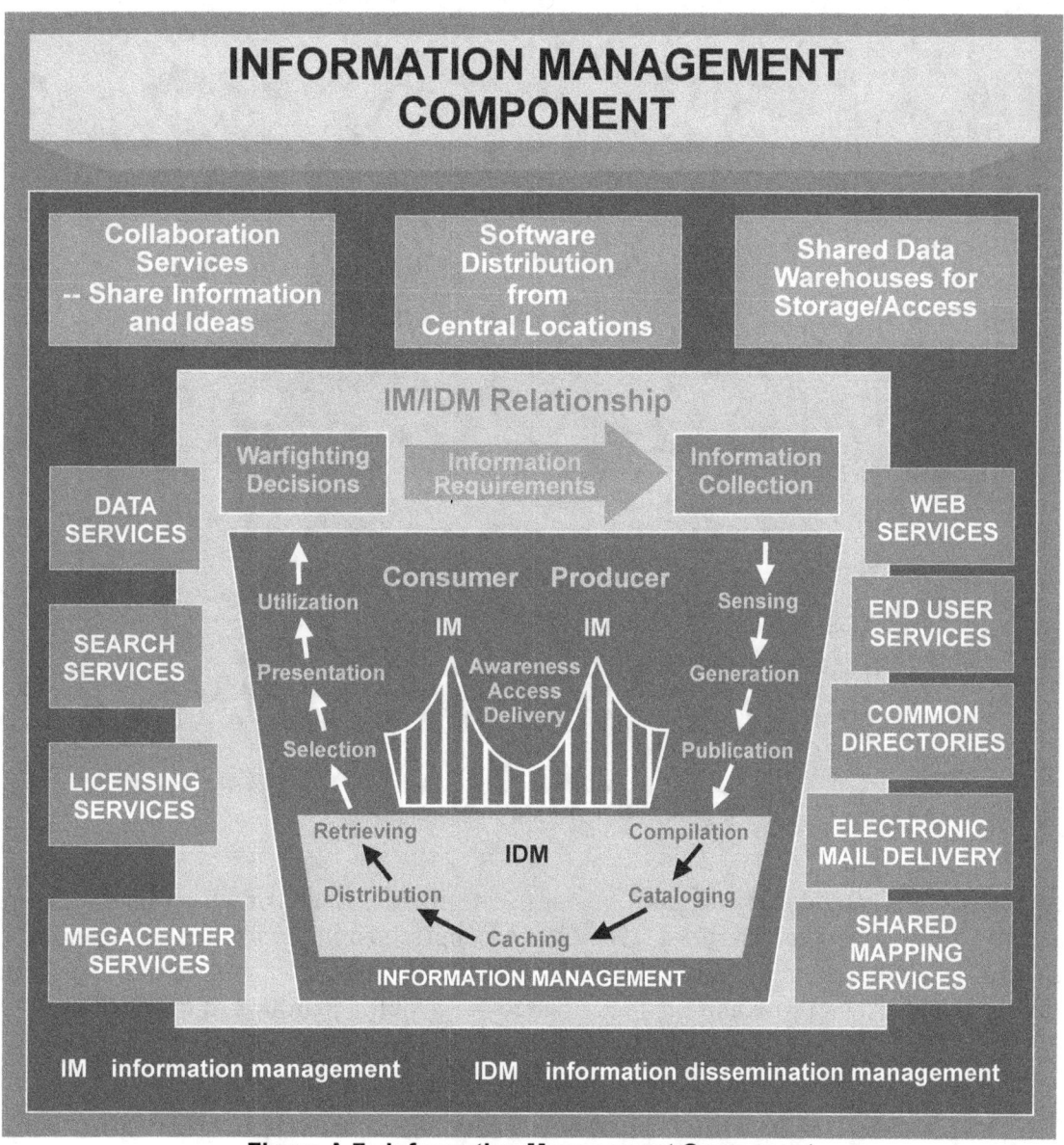

Figure A-7. Information Management Component

8. Foundation Component

The **foundation component** (Figure A-8) includes doctrine, policy, compliance, architectures, testing, electromagnetic spectrum, and host-nation approval. It anchors and

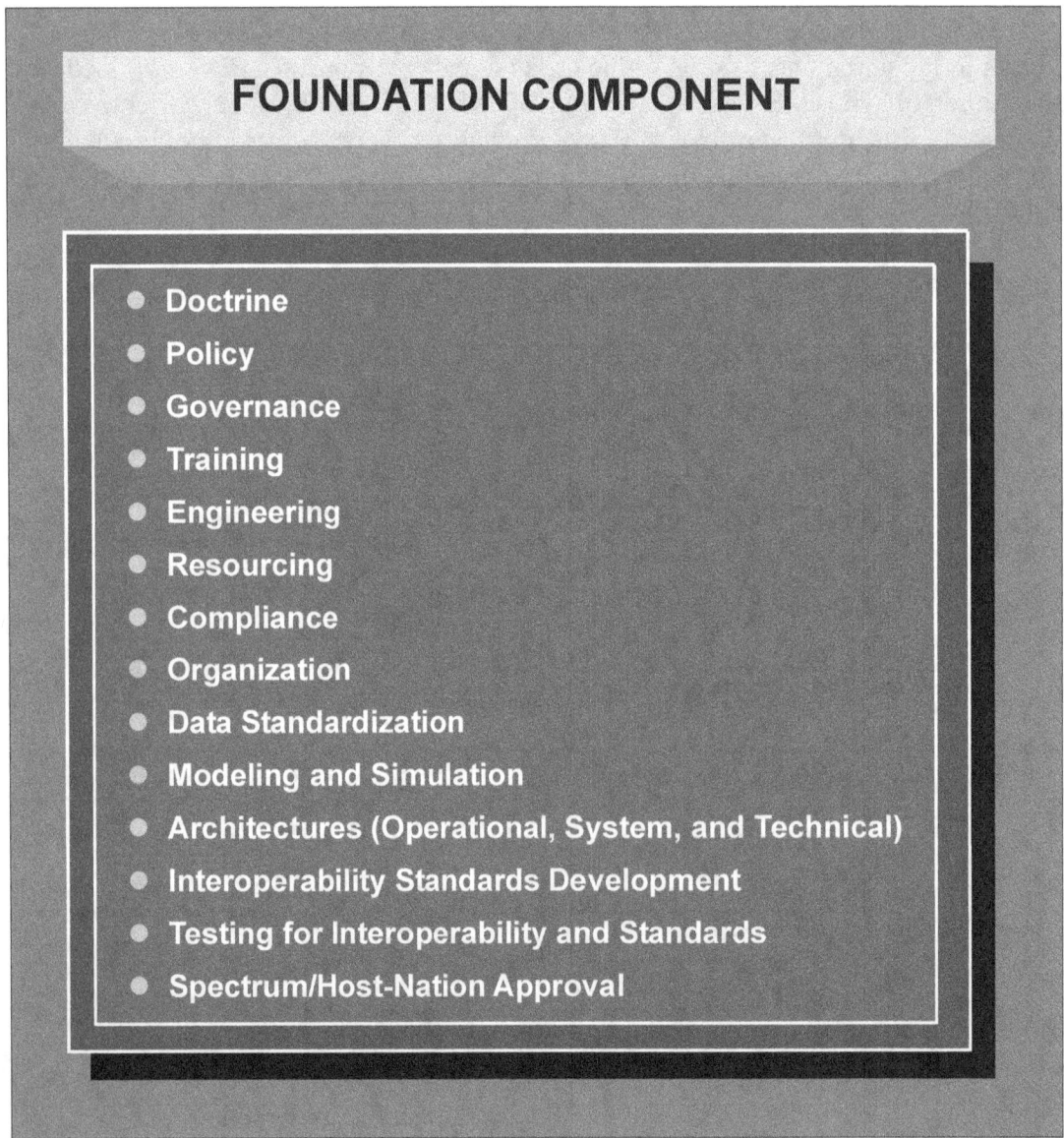

FOUNDATION COMPONENT

- Doctrine
- Policy
- Governance
- Training
- Engineering
- Resourcing
- Compliance
- Organization
- Data Standardization
- Modeling and Simulation
- Architectures (Operational, System, and Technical)
- Interoperability Standards Development
- Testing for Interoperability and Standards
- Spectrum/Host-Nation Approval

Figure A-8. Foundation Component

defines the GIG through policy and standards. It provides the basis for an interoperable, secure DOD networked enterprise. The GIG baseline capability encompasses integrating all DOD requirements — strategic, operational, tactical, and base/post/camp/station/shipboard — providing flexible, assured bandwidth regardless of environment.

APPENDIX B
JOINT FORCE COMMUNICATIONS SYSTEM
ESTIMATE PREPARATION GUIDE

1. General

This appendix provides communications system planners with an outline to assist planning. This outline was adapted from the USJFCOM communications system estimate training guide.

2. Situation

The JFC has received a planning directive (e.g., CCDR's warning order, planning order). Normally, the joint planning group (JPG) has been assembled, and the planning of an operation is ongoing. The communications system planner will develop the communications system estimate by identifying, coordinating, and integrating communications system support into the joint force operation.

REFERENCES: *JP 3-0, JP 3-33, and CJCSM 3122.01A.*

3. Developing the Communications System Estimate Analysis

a. Determine known facts, status, or conditions of communications system elements provided in the commander's planning guidance document (e.g., warning order, planning order, or alert order).

b. Understand the CCDR's mission and proposed operations/tasks to components.

    (1) Mission assigned to the CCDR.

    (2) Required results.

    (3) Actions required to achieve results.

    (4) Location of required results.

    (5) Timing of required results.

    (6) Limitations on freedom of action.

c. Review and describe the communications system situation.

    (1) Characteristics of the operational area; emphasize factors affecting communications system activities.

    (2) Adversary capabilities. Place specific emphasis on communications system matters.

(3) Friendly forces.

(a) Disposition (positions) of major units that have been provided by the combatant command for planning.

(b) Own COAs. State the proposed COAs under consideration.

(c) Probable operations/tactical developments. Review major deployments and communications system preparations necessary in all phases of the proposed campaign/major operation.

(4) The logistic situation. Review known logistic problems that may affect the communications system situation.

(5) The personnel situation. Review known or anticipated personnel problems that may influence the communications system estimate and the selection of a specific COA. Consider the requirement for and availability of JCSE augmentation.

(6) Special features. Special aspects not covered elsewhere that may affect the communications system situation, such as the host nation and its ability and willingness to allow access/operation of communications system assets or the affects of scintillation on long-haul communications

(7) Communications system. Consider line-of-sight communications, SATCOM, UHF SATCOM, ground mobile segment, and DISN interface. Review all military and commercial options.

(a) Administrative communications.

(b) Logistics and medical communications.

(c) Intelligence communications architecture.

(d) COMSEC.

(e) Communications support for combat operations:

1. Joint tactical air operations.

2. Air-to-ground operations.

3. Naval surface fire support operations.

4. Other component-specific communications system.

(f) Communications control and aids for supporting operations.

(g) Interoperability of the communications system, both horizontally and vertically.

(h) Communications required for other activities (video teleconference, etc.).

d. Understand the deception guidance — objective, target, story, if any.

e. Understand the guidance on risk, if any.

f. Understand the desired end state.

g. Provide factors affecting communications.

(1) The topography in the JOA.

(2) The available communications resources.

(3) The communications readiness of available forces.

h. Determine limitations.

(1) Restrictions placed on the JFC.

(a) Constraints. Required actions that limit freedom of action (e.g., conduct air strikes within a specific period of time).

(b) Restraints. Actions the JFC is prohibited from taking (e.g., cannot pursue the adversary across an international border).

(2) Imposed by higher HQ, host nation, alliance/coalition, etc.

(3) Implied by conditions, circumstances — may be described as assumptions.

i. Develop assumptions to replace missing or unknown information. NOTE: Assumptions must be valid (likely to occur) and necessary (essential for continued planning), e.g., sufficient satellite channels/bandwidth availability.

(1) Intelligence related assumptions. See the J-2 (intelligence).

(a) Impact of characteristics of the JOA.

(b) Adversary intentions, probable COAs, vulnerabilities.

(c) Status of friendly support.

(2) Operationally related assumptions. See J-3/plans directorate of a joint staff (J-5) (operations/plans).

(a) Status of forces at probable execution.

(b) Probability of success after the force ratio analysis.

(c) Available time.

(3) Logistic-related assumptions. See the J-4 (logistics).

(a) Logistic status-of-forces at probable execution.

(b) Logistic impact of characteristics of the JOA.

(c) Acquisition plan for extraordinary material and services.

(4) Communications/computer-related assumptions.

(a) Communications status at probable execution.

(b) Determine national/theater-level communications support in coordination with the combatant command J-6.

4. Receive the Joint Force Commander Planning Guidance

The JFC should provide detailed guidance at this point. Planning guidance should be disseminated to J-6 personnel and the joint force components. If needed, ask the J-3/J-5/JFC for any guidance necessary for continued planning.

5. Develop Options for Communications System Support of the Joint Force Commander's Courses of Action

a. Use analytical models or databases to assist in determining requirements and the communications system architecture.

b. For combat operations.

(1) Review the mission analysis and the commander's guidance and intent.

(2) Develop options for communications system support for each COA.

(a) State clearly what is to be accomplished, including phasing of the communications system support to the campaign or operation.

(b) Outline communications system support to the military deception objective and story.

(c) Specify ways (operations) and means (forces) to provide communications system support to accomplish objectives (e.g., attacking adversary centers of gravity).

(d) Outline the major communications system tasks to be performed to support the JFC, including the supporting/supported relationships by phase, and tasks to be accomplished by the supporting organizations and agencies.

(e) Outline the deployment scheme for communications system resources.

(3) Identify force requirements for communications system support.

(4) Describe C2 means and relationships for communications system support.

c. For noncombat operations.

(1) Review the mission analysis and JFC's guidance (e.g., commander's intent).

(2) Develop communications system support options for each COA.

(a) Clearly state what is to be accomplished.

(b) Specify ways (operations) and means (forces) to provide communications system support to accomplish objectives.

(c) Outline the major communications system tasks to be performed to support the JFC, including the supporting/supported relationships by phase, and tasks to be accomplished by the supporting organizations and agencies.

(3) Identify the force requirements for communications system resources.

(4) Describe the C2 means and relationships for communications system support.

6. **Participate in the Course of Action Analysis (Wargaming)**

a. Gather tools.

(1) Identify the adversary and friendly COAs to analyze.

(2) Prepare maps of the JOA with communications system information.

(3) Join the wargaming team -- normally representatives from J-2, J-3, J-4, and J-6.

(4) Depict current adversary dispositions.

b. Identify the available joint forces and augmentation from:

(1) A joint space support team.

(2) DISA.

(3) RSSC.

(4) The Joint Spectrum Center.

(5) JCSE/CJCS controlled assets.

c. List assumptions related to communications system support.

d. Review and/or contribute to the development of known critical events and decision points — specified and implied tasks and decisions that must be made to ensure timely execution and synchronization of resources.

e. Review or contribute to selecting the wargame method. Generally allow action/reaction/counteraction sequence and assessment.

f. Participate in wargaming.

(1) Provide a perspective on communications system requirements related to friendly operations.

(2) Determine communications system objectives and integrate communications system support within the context of the COA under consideration.

(3) Identify potential adjustments to the required friendly force deployment to ensure communications system resources for the COA under consideration.

(4) Contribute refinements or modifications to the COAs and to the concepts for communications system support.

(5) Contribute to branches, sequels, or additional critical events — additional operations that might be required as a result of adversary actions not previously anticipated.

(6) Contribute to critical information.

(7) Contribute to COA(s) for the associated military deception plan.

(8) Identify major communications system tasks to the Service/functional components.

(9) Estimate the duration of communications system support requirements.

(10) Identify major requirements for communications system support of operations.

(11) Develop communications system input/information for the synchronization matrix and decision support template.

(12) Identify advantages, disadvantages of friendly COAs from the J-6 perspective of supportability.

g. Repeat for all combinations of adversary and friendly COAs.

7. **Participate in the Course of Action Comparison**

Test the validity of each COA.

a. Tests for suitability.

(1) Does it accomplish the mission?

(2) Does it meet the commander's intent?

(3) Does it accomplish all the essential tasks?

(4) Does it meet the conditions for the end state?

(5) Does it take into consideration the adversary and friendly centers of gravity?

b. Preliminary test for feasibility.

(1) Does the JFC have the force structure (means) to carry it out? The COA is feasible if it can be carried out with the forces, support, and technology available, within the constraints of the physical environment, and against the expected enemy opposition.

(2) Although this process occurs during COA analysis and the test at this time is preliminary, it may be possible to declare a COA infeasible (e.g., resources

are obviously insufficient). However, it may be possible to fill shortfalls by requesting additional support through the geographic combatant command.

    c. Preliminary test for acceptability.

        (1) Does it contain unacceptable risks?

        (2) Does it take into account the limitations placed on the JFC (constraints [must do] and restraints [cannot do])? A COA is considered acceptable if the estimated results are worth the estimated costs. The basis of this test consists of an estimation of friendly losses in forces, time, position, and opportunity.

        (3) Acceptability is considered from the perspective of the JFC and the CCDR, by reviewing the JFC's contribution to the CCDR's objective.

        (4) COAs are reconciled with external constraints, particularly rules of engagement.

        (5) Requires visualization of execution of the COA against each adversary capability. Although this process occurs during the COA analysis and the test at this time is preliminary, it may be possible to declare a COA unacceptable if it violates the JFC's definition of acceptable risk.

    d. Test for differences or variety. Is it fundamentally different from other COAs? They can be different when considering:

        (1) Focus or direction of the main effort.

        (2) Scheme of maneuver (land, air, maritime, and special operations).

        (3) Primary mechanism for mission accomplishment.

        (4) Task organization.

        (5) Use of reserves.

    e. Preliminary test for completeness. Does it answer the questions who, what, when, where, why, and how?

    f. Provide forces and deployment requirements to the joint force deployment cell.

    g. Provide conclusions.

        (1) State whether the JFC's mission is supportable from a J-6 perspective.

(2) State which COA can best be supported from a J-6 standpoint.

(3) Identify the major communications system deficiencies and make recommendations to reduce or eliminate them.

(a) Are CJCS-controlled assets required?

(b) Is JCSE required?

(c) Are en route communications required?

h. Ensure that recommendations are coordinated with the J-6-equivalent at each Service/functional component and the supported combatant command J-6.

i. Recommend a COA from a J-6 perspective.

8. Receive the Joint Force Commander's Decision on the Course of Action

The JFC may select or modify the recommended COA. Based on that decision, the JFC's estimate document (or slides) will normally be sent or briefed to the supported CCDR for approval.

9. Prepare and Submit Annex K (communications supplement/instructions) to the Joint Force Plan/Order

Note: If steps 1-6 above were completed, most of the information needed for annex K is now available.

a. Identify the communications system functions required to support the proposed joint operation.

(1) Collect information based on the stated need and convert that information into the required format for the annex K.

(2) Coordinate, as necessary, with the combatant command J-6 and the J-6-equivalents at the Service/functional components.

(3) Provide the information/annex K to the focal point for the OPLAN/OPORD, normally the JPG.

(4) Disseminate essential information regarding communications system and networks throughout the joint force, as required.

(5) Ensure all active and passive communications system support related security measures are in effect to deny the adversary access to friendly information (e.g., COMSEC, INFOSEC, computer security).

b. Identify applicable planning guidelines/principles for the communications system support. Consider:

(1) The integration of organic and non-organic military and commercial communications systems, so the interfaces are transparent and the systems reliable.

(2) Plan/coordinate for the replacement of JCSE IAW USJFCOM instruction 2014.1.

(3) Horizontal and vertical C2 linkages.

(4) A balance between "push" and "pull" systems to meet the information needs of the joint force.

(5) Planning principles.

(a) Modular communications system packages.

(b) Interoperable procedures, training, and equipment that permits the internal and external exchange of information.

1. What interfaces are required for multinational forces?

2. Can the Joint Interoperability Test Command assist with potential interoperability solutions?

(c) The use of liaison officers/teams to provide a means to facilitate interoperability during different tactical phases of an operation.

(d) The flexibility to allow for changes in mission or to accommodate a diversity of communications schemes and equipment.

(e) Balance the need for redundancy and flexibility with the available assets.

(f) Survivable communications system architecture that includes a diversity of communications routes, hardening and protection of equipment and communications sites, and availability of alternate modular communications system packages.

(g) Redundancy that provides diversity of paths over multiple media means, with available replacement systems and repair parts. The goal is timely, reliable information flow.

(h) Use of available commercial networks.

<u>1.</u> What special interfaces are required?

<u>2.</u> What are the power requirements?

<u>3.</u> Are additional funds required?

(i) Electromagnetic spectrum management to avoid harmful EMI and hazards of electromagnetic radiation to ordinance (through host nation coordination and analysis and evaluation of potential electromagnetic spectrum conflicts as part of the JOPES process, ongoing missions and training) and to protect the most critical communications functions through coordination and distribution of a JRFL.

(j) Security must account for users' information requirements, the vulnerability of communications system to interception, exploitation, disruption, and destruction by the adversary.

(k) IA principles must be included to minimize the threats posed by computer viruses, hackers, and denial of service attacks.

c. Consider equipment and system characteristics necessary for proposed operations. The communications system should be designed to be interoperable, agile, trusted, and shared.

d. **Refine the concept of communications system support**

(1) Determine/refine command IERs.

(a) Should be based on the consolidated requirements of the JFC.

(b) Consider communications system support to other operations/functions (e.g., information operations, military deception, military information support operations, fire support systems, airspace management, air defense).

(c) Consider the battle rhythm of the staff, reporting times, and times of critical planning meetings.

(2) Match communications system IERs with communications system capabilities and assets.

(3) Conduct communications system planning and engineering. Design the communications system architecture.

(a) Use available automated planning tools (e.g., JNMS).

(b) Define the architecture in terms of communications system nodes and associated communications system, grouped into modular packages keyed to operational mission phases and deployment schedules.

(c) Describe the interconnection of modular packages to communications system and the resulting communications system networks. Consider using an automated planning tool, then comparing results with mission phases and deployment schedules.

(d) Include description of supporting SYSCON centers, technical control centers, and technical control facilities.

(e) Upon validation of the requirements, input applicable information to the joint force point of contact for the TPFDD for forwarding to the supported combatant command.

(4) Program the activation of communications system links and networks.

(5) Plan for management of the electromagnetic spectrum.

(a) Use allocations, allotments, and assignments of frequencies and frequency ranges.

(b) Ensure that frequencies have electromagnetic compatibility.

(c) Plan to request monitoring of the electromagnetic spectrum for EMI (as required).

(d) Develop appropriate joint CEOI.

(6) Plan for security of communications system and networks — INFOSEC.

(a) Transmission security.

(b) Cryptographic security.

(c) Emission security.

(7) Coordinate plan with meteorology and oceanographic observations.

e. Prepare and submit annex K (communications supplement/instructions) to the OPLAN/OPORD.

(1) Use available automated planning/annex preparation tools.

(2) Include joint CEOI and related instructions.

Intentionally Blank

APPENDIX C
REFERENCES

The following references support the doctrinal concepts described in JP 6-0.

1. Department of Defense Publications

a. DODD 4630.05, *Interoperability and Supportability of Information Technology (IT) and National Security Systems (NSS)*.

b. DODD 5105.19, *Defense Information Systems Agency (DISA)*.

c. DODI 4630.8, *Procedures for Interoperability and Supportability of Information Technology (IT) and National Security Systems (NSS)*.

2. Chairman of the Joint Chiefs of Staff Publications

a. CJCSI 2700.01A, *International Military Agreements for Rationalization, Standardization, and Interoperability (RSI) Between the United States, Its Allies, and Other Friendly Nations*.

b. CJCSI 3155.01, *Global Command and Control System-Joint (GCCS-J) Operational Framework Policy*.

c. CJCSI 3320.01B, *Electromagnetic Spectrum Use in Joint Military Operations*.

d. CJCSI 3320.03A, *Joint Communications Electronics Operation Instructions*.

e. CJCSI 5721.01D, *The Defense Message System and Associated Legacy Message Processing Systems*.

f. CJCSI 6211.02C, *Defense Information System Network (DISN): Policy and Responsibilities*.

g. CJCSI 6212.01E, *Interoperability and Supportability of Information Technology and National Security Systems*.

h. CJCSI 6215.01C, *Policy for Department of Defense Voice Networks with Real Time Services (RTS)*.

i. CJCSI 6241.04B *Policy and Procedures for Using United States Message Text Formatting*.

j. CJCSI 6250.01C, *Satellite Communications*.

k. CJCSI 6251.01B, *Ultrahigh Frequency (UHF) Satellite Communications Demand Assigned Multiple Access Requirements*.

l. CJCSI 6510.01E, *Information Assurance (IA) and Computer Network Defense (CND)*.

m. CJCSI 6510.06A, *Communications Security Releases to Foreign Nations*.

n. CJCSI 6731.01B, *Global Command and Control System Security Policy*.

o. CJCSI 6740.01B, *Military Telecommunications Agreements and Arrangements Between the United States and Regional Defense Organizations or Friendly Foreign Nations*.

p. CJCSM 3150.01B, *Joint Reporting Structure General Instructions*.

q. CJCSM 3150.07C, *Joint Reporting Structure Communications Status*.

r. CJCSM 3320.01B, *Joint Operations in the Electromagnetic Battlespace*.

s. CJCSM 3320.02B, *Joint Spectrum Interference Resolution (JSIR) Procedures*.

t. CJCSM 6120.01D, *Joint Multi-Tactical Data Link (TDL) Operating Procedures*.

u. CJCSM *6231* series, *Manual for Employing Joint Tactical Communications*.

v. CJCSM 6510.01A, *Information Assurance (IA) and Computer Network Defense (CND)*.

3. **Joint Publications**

a. JP 1, *Doctrine for the Armed Forces of the United States*.

b. JP 3-0, *Joint Operations*.

c. JP 3-13, *Information Operations*.

d. JP 3-16, *Multinational Operations*.

e. JP 5-0, *Joint Operation Planning*.

4. **Multi-Service Publication**

FM 6-02.85/MCRP 3-40.2A/NWP 3-13.1.16/AFTTP(I) 3-2.22, *Multi-Service Tactics, Techniques, and Procedures for Joint Task Force Information Management*.

APPENDIX D
ADMINISTRATIVE INSTRUCTIONS

1. User Comments

Users in the field are highly encouraged to submit comments on this publication to: Commander, USJFCOM, Joint Warfighting Center, ATTN: Doctrine and Education Group, 116 Lake View Parkway, Suffolk, VA 23435-2697. These comments should address content (accuracy, usefulness, consistency, and organization), writing, and appearance.

2. Authorship

The lead agent and Joint Staff doctrine sponsor for this publication is the Director for Battlespace Communications System (J-6).

3. Supersession

This publication supersedes JP 6-0, *Joint Communications System,* 20 March 2006.

4. Change Recommendations

a. Recommendations for urgent changes to this publication should be submitted:

TO: JOINT STAFF WASHINGTON DC//J6//
INFO: JOINT STAFF WASHINGTON DC//J7-JEDD//
          CDRUSJFCOM SUFFOLK VA//DOC GP//

Routine changes should be submitted electronically to Commander, Joint Warfighting Center, Doctrine and Education Group and info the Lead Agent and the Director for Operational Plans and Joint Force Development J-7/JEDD via the CJCS JEL at http://www.dtic.mil/doctrine.

b. When a Joint Staff directorate submits a proposal to the CJCS that would change source document information reflected in this publication, that directorate will include a proposed change to this publication as an enclosure to its proposal. The Military Services and other organizations are requested to notify the Joint Staff/J-7 when changes to source documents reflected in this publication are initiated.

c. Record of Changes:

CHANGE NUMBER	COPY NUMBER	DATE OF CHANGE	DATE ENTERED	POSTED BY	REMARKS

5. Distribution of Publications

Local reproduction is authorized and access to unclassified publications is unrestricted. However, access to and reproduction authorization for classified joint publications must be in accordance with DOD 5200.1-R, *Information Security Program*.

6. Distribution of Electronic Publications

a. Joint Staff J-7 will not print copies of joint publications for distribution. Electronic versions are available on JDEIS at https://jdeis.js.mil (NIPRNET), and https://jdeis.js.smil.mil (SIPRNET) and on the JEL at http://www.dtic.mil/doctrine (NIPRNET).

b. Only approved joint publications and joint test publications are releasable outside the combatant commands, Services, and Joint Staff. Release of any classified joint publication to foreign governments or foreign nationals must be requested through the local embassy (Defense Attaché Office) to DIA, Defense Foreign Liaison/IE-3, 200 MacDill Blvd., Bolling AFB, Washington, DC 20340-5100.

c. CD-ROM. Upon request of a JDDC member, the Joint Staff J-7 will produce and deliver one CD-ROM with current joint publications.

ABCS	Army Battle Command System
ACP	Allied communications publication
AFTTP(I)	Air Force tactics, techniques, and procedures (instruction)
AMHS	automated message handling system
AOR	area of responsibility
ASD(NII)	Assistant Secretary of Defense (Networks and Information Integration)
bps	bits per second
C2	command and control
CCB	configuration control board
CCDR	combatant commander
CCEB	Combined Communications-Electronics Board
CCIR	commander's critical information requirement
CDP	commander's dissemination policy
CDRUSSTRATCOM	Commander, United States Strategic Command
CEOI	communications-electronics operating instructions
CERT	computer emergency response team
CFC	Combined Forces Command, Korea
CIO	chief information officer
CJCS	Chairman of the Joint Chiefs of Staff
CJCSI	Chairman of the Joint Chiefs of Staff instruction
CJCSM	Chairman of the Joint Chiefs of Staff manual
CND	computer network defense
COA	course of action
COCOM	combatant command (command authority)
COI	community of interest
COMSEC	communications security
CONUS	continental United States
COP	common operational picture
DAA	designated approving authority
DCO	Defense Connect Online
DIA	Defense Intelligence Agency
DISA	Defense Information Systems Agency
DISA-LO	Defense Information Systems Agency-liaison officer
DISN	Defense Information Systems Network
DJS	Director, Joint Staff
DOD	Department of Defense
DODD	Department of Defense directive
DODI	Department of Defense instruction
DODIIS	Department of Defense Intelligence Information System
DRSN	Defense Red Switched Network
DSCS	Defense Satellite Communications System

DSN	Defense Switched Network
DSTS-G	Defense Information Systems Network (DISN) Satellite Transmission Services - Global
EHF	extremely high frequency
EMI	electromagnetic interference
EW	electronic warfare
EWCC	electronic warfare coordination cell
FCC	Federal Communications Commission
FLTSATCOM	fleet satellite communications
FM	field manual (Army)
FMO	frequency management office
GAR	gateway access request
GBS	Global Broadcast Service
GCC	geographic combatant commander
GCCS	Global Command and Control System
GCCS-J	Global Command and Control System-Joint
GCM	Global Information Grid (GIG) Content Management
GCSS-J	Global Combat Support System-Joint
GEM	Global Information Grid (GIG) Enterprise Management
GIG	Global Information Grid
GNA	Global Information Grid (GIG) Network Assurance
GNC	global network operations (NETOPS) center
GNCC	global network operations (NETOPS) control center
GNSC	global network operations (NETOPS) support center
GND	Global Information Grid (GIG) Network Defense
GSSC	global satellite communications (SATCOM) support center
HF	high frequency
HQ	headquarters
IA	information assurance
IAVM	information assurance vulnerability management
IAW	in accordance with
IC	intelligence community
IDM	information dissemination management
IER	information exchange requirement
IGO	intergovernmental organization
IM	information management
IMSP	information management support plan
INFOCON	information operations condition
INFOSEC	information security
INMARSAT	international maritime satellite
IO	information operations

IPS	Interim Polar System
IS	information superiority
ISR	intelligence, surveillance, and reconnaissance
IT	information technology
J-2	intelligence directorate of a joint staff
J-3	operations directorate of a joint staff
J-4	logistics directorate of a joint staff
J-5	plans directorate of a joint staff
J-6	communications system directorate of a joint staff
JCCA	joint combat capability assessment
JCEWS	joint force commander's electronic warfare staff
JCISA	Joint Command Information Systems Activity
JCS	Joint Chiefs of Staff
JCSE	joint communications support element
JDN	joint data network
JFC	joint force commander
JFCC NW	Joint Functional Component Command for Network Warfare
JFMO	joint frequency management office
JIMB	joint information management board
JNCC	joint network operations (NETOPS) control center
JNMS	joint network management system
JOA	joint operations area
JOC	joint operations center
JOPES	Joint Operation Planning and Execution System
JP	joint publication
JPG	joint planning group
JRFL	joint restricted frequency list
JRSOI	joint reception, staging, onward movement, and integration
JSME	joint spectrum management element
JTF	joint task force
JTF-GNO	Joint Task Force-Global Network Operations
JWICS	Joint Worldwide Intelligence Communications System
Ka	Kurtz-above band
kbps	kilobits per second
Ku	Kurtz-under band
LAN	local area network
LPD	low probability of detection
LPI	low probability of intercept
M&S	modeling and simulation
MARS	Military Auxiliary Radio System
MCEB	Military Communications-Electronics Board
MCRP	Marine Corps reference publication

MILDEP	Military Department
MWR	morale, welfare, and recreation
NATO	North Atlantic Treaty Organization
NCC	National Coordinating Center
NCCS	Nuclear Command and Control System
NCES	Net-Centric Enterprise Services
NCS	National Communications System
NETOPS	network operations
NGA	National Geospatial-Intelligence Agency
NGO	nongovernmental organization
NIPRNET	Non-Secure Internet Protocol Router Network
NMCC	National Military Command Center
NMCS	National Military Command System
NOSC	network operations and security center
NSA	National Security Agency
NSEP	national security emergency preparedness
NSG	National System for Geospatial Intelligence
NSS	national security system
NSTAC	National Security Telecommunications Advisory Committee
NTIA	National Telecommunications and Information Administration
NWP	Navy warfare publication
OGA	other government agency
OPCON	operational control
OPLAN	operation plan
OPORD	operation order
OPSEC	operations security
OSD	Office of the Secretary of Defense
RF	radio frequency
RSC	regional service center
RSSC	regional satellite communications (SATCOM) support center
RSSC-LO	regional satellite communications support center liaison officer
SA	situational awareness
SAR	site access request
SATCOM	satellite communications
SCI	sensitive compartmented information
SecDef	Secretary of Defense
SHF	super-high frequency
SIPRNET	SECRET Internet Protocol Router Network

SJFHQ	standing joint force headquarters
SLA	service level agreement
SOM	satellite communications (SATCOM) operational manager
SSE	satellite communications (SATCOM) systems expert
STEP	standardized tactical entry point
SYSCON	systems control
TACSAT	tactical satellite
TBMCS	theater battle management core system
TDL	tactical data link
TIM	theater information management
TJTN	theater joint tactical network
TNC	theater network operations (NETOPS) center
TNCC	theater network operations (NETOPS) control center
TPFDD	time-phased force and deployment data
TTP	tactics, techniques, and procedures
UFO	ultrahigh frequency follow-on
UHF	ultrahigh frequency
UNC	United Nations Command
USC	United States Code
USCYBERCOM	United States Cyber Command
USD(I)	Under Secretary of Defense for Intelligence
USFK	United States Forces, Korea
USJFCOM	United States Joint Forces Command
USNORTHCOM	United States Northern Command
USSTRATCOM	United States Strategic Command
VTC	video teleconferencing
WAN	wide-area network
WGS	Wideband Global Satellite Communications (SATCOM)

PART II — TERMS AND DEFINITIONS

Unless otherwise annotated, this publication is the proponent for all terms and definitions found in the glossary. Upon approval, JP 1-02, *Department of Defense Dictionary of Military and Associated Terms*, will reflect this publication as the source document for these terms and definitions.

architecture. A framework or structure that portrays relationships among all the elements of the subject force, system, or activity. (JP 1-02. SOURCE: JP 3-05)

command and control system. The facilities, equipment, communications, procedures, and personnel essential to a commander for planning, directing, and controlling operations of assigned and attached forces pursuant to the missions assigned. (JP 1-02. SOURCE: JP 6-0)

commonality. A quality that applies to materiel or systems: a. possessing like and interchangeable characteristics enabling each to be utilized, or operated and maintained, by personnel trained on the others without additional specialized training; b. having interchangeable repair parts and/or components; and c. applying to consumable items interchangeably equivalent without adjustment. (Approved for incorporation into JP 1-02 with JP 6-0 as the source JP.)

common operational picture. A single identical display of relevant information shared by more than one command. A common operational picture facilitates collaborative planning and assists all echelons to achieve situational awareness. Also called COP. (JP 1-02. SOURCE: JP 3-0)

communicate. To use any means or method to convey information of any kind from one person or place to another. (JP 1-02. SOURCE: JP 6-0)

communication operation instructions. None. (Approved for removal from JP 1-02.)

communications net. None. (Approved for removal from JP 1-02.)

communications network. An organization of stations capable of intercommunications, but not necessarily on the same channel. (JP 1-02. SOURCE: JP 6-0)

communications satellite. An orbiting vehicle, which relays signals between communications stations. There are two types: a. active communications satellite —A satellite that receives, regenerates, and retransmits signals between stations; b. passive communications satellite — A satellite which reflects communications signals between stations. Also called COMSAT. (JP 1-02. SOURCE: JP 6-0)

communications security. The protection resulting from all measures designed to deny unauthorized persons information of value that might be derived from the possession and study of telecommunications, or to mislead unauthorized persons in their interpretation of the results of such possession and study. Also called COMSEC. (JP 1-02. SOURCE: JP 6-0)

communications system. None. (Approved for removal from JP 1-02.)

computer network defense. Actions taken to protect, monitor, analyze, detect, and respond to unauthorized activity within the Department of Defense information systems and computer networks. Also called CND. (JP 1-02. SOURCE: JP 6-0)

computer security. The protection resulting from all measures to deny unauthorized access and exploitation of friendly computer systems. Also called COMPUSEC. (JP 1-02. SOURCE: JP 6-0)

configuration management. A discipline applying technical and administrative direction and surveillance to: (1) identify and document the functional and physical characteristics of a configuration item; (2) control changes to those characteristics; and (3) record and report changes to processing and implementation status. (Approved for incorporation into JP 1-02 with JP 6-0 as the source JP.)

control. 1. Authority that may be less than full command exercised by a commander over part of the activities of subordinate or other organizations. 2. In mapping, charting, and photogrammetry, a collective term for a system of marks or objects on the Earth or on a map or a photograph, whose positions or elevations (or both) have been or will be determined. 3. Physical or psychological pressures exerted with the intent to assure that an agent or group will respond as directed. 4. An indicator governing the distribution and use of documents, information, or material. Such indicators are the subject of intelligence community agreement and are specifically defined in appropriate regulations. (Approved for incorporation into JP 1-02 with JP 1 as the source JP for Definition 1.)

critical infrastructure protection. Actions taken to prevent, remediate, or mitigate the risks resulting from vulnerabilities of critical infrastructure assets. Depending on the risk, these actions could include: changes in tactics, techniques, or procedures; adding redundancy; selection of another asset; isolation or hardening; guarding, etc. Also called CIP. (JP 1-02. SOURCE: JP 3-28)

cryptosecurity. None (Approved for removal from JP 1-02.)

cyberspace. A global domain within the information environment consisting of the interdependent network of information technology infrastructures, including the Internet, telecommunications networks, computer systems, and embedded processors and controllers. (JP 1-02. SOURCE: CJCS CM-0363-08)

data link. None. (Approved for removal from JP 1-02.)

decrypt. None. (Approved for removal from JP 1-02.)

Defense Information Systems Network. Integrated network, centrally managed and configured to provide long-haul information transfer services for all Department of Defense activities. It is an information transfer utility designed to provide dedicated point-to-point, switched voice and data, imagery, and video teleconferencing services. Also called DISN. (Approved for incorporation into JP 1-02 with JP 6-0 as the source JP.)

Defense Switched Network. Component of the Defense Communications System that handles Department of Defense voice, data, and video communications. Also called DSN. (Approved for incorporation into JP 1-02 with JP 6-0 as the source JP.)

electromagnetic spectrum management. Planning, coordinating, and managing joint use of the electromagnetic spectrum through operational, engineering, and administrative procedures. The objective of spectrum management is to enable electronic systems to perform their functions in the intended environment without causing or suffering unacceptable interference. (JP 1-02. SOURCE: JP 6-0)

emission security. The component of communications security that results from all measures taken to deny unauthorized persons information of value that might be derived from intercept and analysis of compromising emanations from crypto-equipment and telecommunications systems. (JP 1-02. SOURCE: JP 6-0)

frequency management. The requesting, recording, deconfliction of and issuance of authorization to use frequencies (operate electromagnetic spectrum dependent systems) coupled with monitoring and interference resolution processes. (JP 1-02. SOURCE: JP 6-0)

garble. None. (Approved for removal from JP 1-02.)

Global Combat Support System-Joint. The primary information technology application used to provide automation support to the joint logistician. Also called GCSS-J. (JP 1-02. SOURCE: JP 4-0)

Global Command and Control System. A deployable command and control system supporting forces for joint and multinational operations across the range of military operations with compatible, interoperable, and integrated communications systems. Also called GCCS. (JP 1-02. SOURCE: JP 6-0)

Global Information Grid. The globally interconnected, end-to-end set of information capabilities, associated processes for collecting, processing, storing, disseminating, and managing information on demand to warfighters, policy makers, and support personnel. The Global Information Grid includes owned and leased communications and computing systems and services, software (including applications), data, security services, other associated services and National Security Systems. Also called GIG. (Approved for incorporation into JP 1-02.)

Global Network Operations Center. United States Strategic Command operational element responsible for providing global satellite communications system status; maintaining global situational awareness to include each combatant commander's planned and current operations as well as contingency plans; supporting radio frequency interference resolution management; supporting satellite anomaly resolution and management; facilitating satellite communications interface to the defense information infrastructure; and managing the regional satellite communications support centers. Also called GNC. (JP 1-02. SOURCE: JP 6-0)

information assurance. Measures that protect and defend information and information systems by ensuring their availability, integrity, authentication, confidentiality, and nonrepudiation. This includes providing for restoration of information systems by incorporating protection, detection, and reaction capabilities. Also called IA. (JP 1-02. SOURCE: JP 3-13)

information environment. The aggregate of individuals, organizations, and systems that collect, process, disseminate, or act on information. (JP 1-02. SOURCE: JP 3-13)

information superiority. The operational advantage derived from the ability to collect, process, and disseminate an uninterrupted flow of information while exploiting or denying an adversary's ability to do the same. See also information operations. (JP 1-02. SOURCE: JP 3-13)

interagency coordination. Within the context of Department of Defense involvement, the coordination that occurs between elements of Department of Defense, and engaged US Government agencies for the purpose of achieving an objective. (JP 1-02. SOURCE: JP 3-0.)

interconnection. None. (Approved for removal from JP 1-02.)

interface. None. (Approved for removal from JP 1-02.)

interoperability. 1. The ability to operate in synergy in the execution of assigned tasks. 2. The condition achieved among communications-electronics systems or items of communications-electronics equipment when information or services can be exchanged directly and satisfactorily between them and/or their users. The degree of interoperability should be defined when referring to specific cases. (Approved for incorporation into JP 1-02 with JP 3-0, and JP 6-0 as the source publication for Definition 1, and 2 respectively.)

joint communications network. The aggregation of all the joint communications systems in a theater. The joint communications network includes the joint multi-channel trunking and switching system and the joint command and control communications system(s). Also called JCN. (Approved for incorporation into JP 1-02 with JP 6-0 as the source JP.)

joint network operations control center. An element of the J-6 established to support a joint force commander. The joint network operations control center serves as the single control agency for the management and direction of the joint force communications systems. The joint network operations control center may include plans and operations, administration, system control, and frequency management sections. Also called JNCC. (JP 1-02. SOURCE: JP 6-0)

joint restricted frequency list. A time and geographically-oriented listing of TABOO, PROTECTED, and GUARDED functions, nets, and frequencies. It should be limited to the minimum number of frequencies necessary for friendly forces to accomplish objectives. Also called JRFL. (JP 1-02. SOURCE: JP 3-13.1)

minimize. A condition wherein normal message and telephone traffic is drastically reduced in order that messages connected with an actual or simulated emergency shall not be delayed. (JP 1-02. SOURCE: JP 6-0)

National Communications System. The telecommunications system that results from the technical and operational integration of the separate telecommunications systems of the several executive branch departments and agencies having a significant telecommunications capability. Also called NCS. (JP 1-02. SOURCE: JP 6-0)

National Military Command System. The priority component of the Global Command and Control System designed to support the President, Secretary of Defense, and Joint Chiefs of Staff in the exercise of their responsibilities. Also called NMCS. (JP 1-02. SOURCE: JP 6-0)

network operations. Activities conducted to operate and defend the Global Information Grid. Also called NETOPS. (JP 1-02. SOURCE: JP 6-0).

node. 1. A location in a mobility system where a movement requirement is originated, processed for onward movement, or terminated. 2. In communications and computer systems, the physical location that provides terminating, switching, and gateway access services to support information exchange. 3. An element of a system that represents a person, place, or physical thing. (Approved for incorporation into JP 1-02 with JP 3-17, JP 6-0, and JP 3-0 as the source publication for Definition 1, 2, and 3 respectively.)

physical security. 1. That part of security concerned with physical measures designed to safeguard personnel; to prevent unauthorized access to equipment, installations, material, and documents; and to safeguard them against espionage, sabotage, damage, and theft. 2. In communications security, the component that results from all physical measures necessary to safeguard classified equipment, material, and documents from access thereto or observation thereof by unauthorized persons. (Approved for incorporation into JP 1-02 with JP 3-0, and JP 6-0 as the source publication for Definition 1, and 2 respectively.)

receipt. None. (Approved for removal from JP 1-02.)

SECRET Internet Protocol Router Network. The worldwide SECRET-level packet switch network that uses high-speed internet protocol routers and high-capacity Defense Information Systems Network circuitry. Also called SIPRNET. (JP 1-02. SOURCE: JP 6-0)

signal operating instructions. A series of orders issued for technical control and coordination of the signal communication activities of a command. In Marine Corps usage, these instructions are designated communication operation instructions. (Approved for replacement of "signal operation instructions" in JP 1-02.)

standardization. The process by which the Department of Defense achieves the closest practicable cooperation among the Services and Department of Defense agencies for the most efficient use of research, development, and production resources, and agrees to adopt on the broadest possible basis the use of: a. common or compatible operational, administrative, and logistic procedures; b. common or compatible technical procedures and criteria; c. common, compatible, or interchangeable supplies, components, weapons, or equipment; and, d. common or compatible tactical doctrine with corresponding organizational compatibility. (JP 1-02. SOURCE: JP 4-02)

systems architecture. None. (Approved for removal from JP 1-02.)

tactical data link. A Joint Staff-approved, standardized communication link suitable for transmission of digital information. Tactical digital information links interface two or more command and control or weapons systems via a single or multiple network architecture and multiple communication media for exchange of tactical information. Also called TDL. (Approved for replacement of "tactical digital information link" and its definition in JP 1-02.)

telecommunications. Any transmission, emission, or reception of signs, signals, writings, images, sounds, or information of any nature by wire, radio, visual, or other electromagnetic systems. (Approved for replacement of "telecommunication" in JP 1-02.)

teleconference. None. (Approved for removal from JP 1-02.)

transmission security. The component of communications security that results from all measures designed to protect transmissions from interception and exploitation by means other than cryptanalysis. (JP 1-02. SOURCE: JP 6-0)

Intentionally Blank

JOINT DOCTRINE PUBLICATIONS HIERARCHY

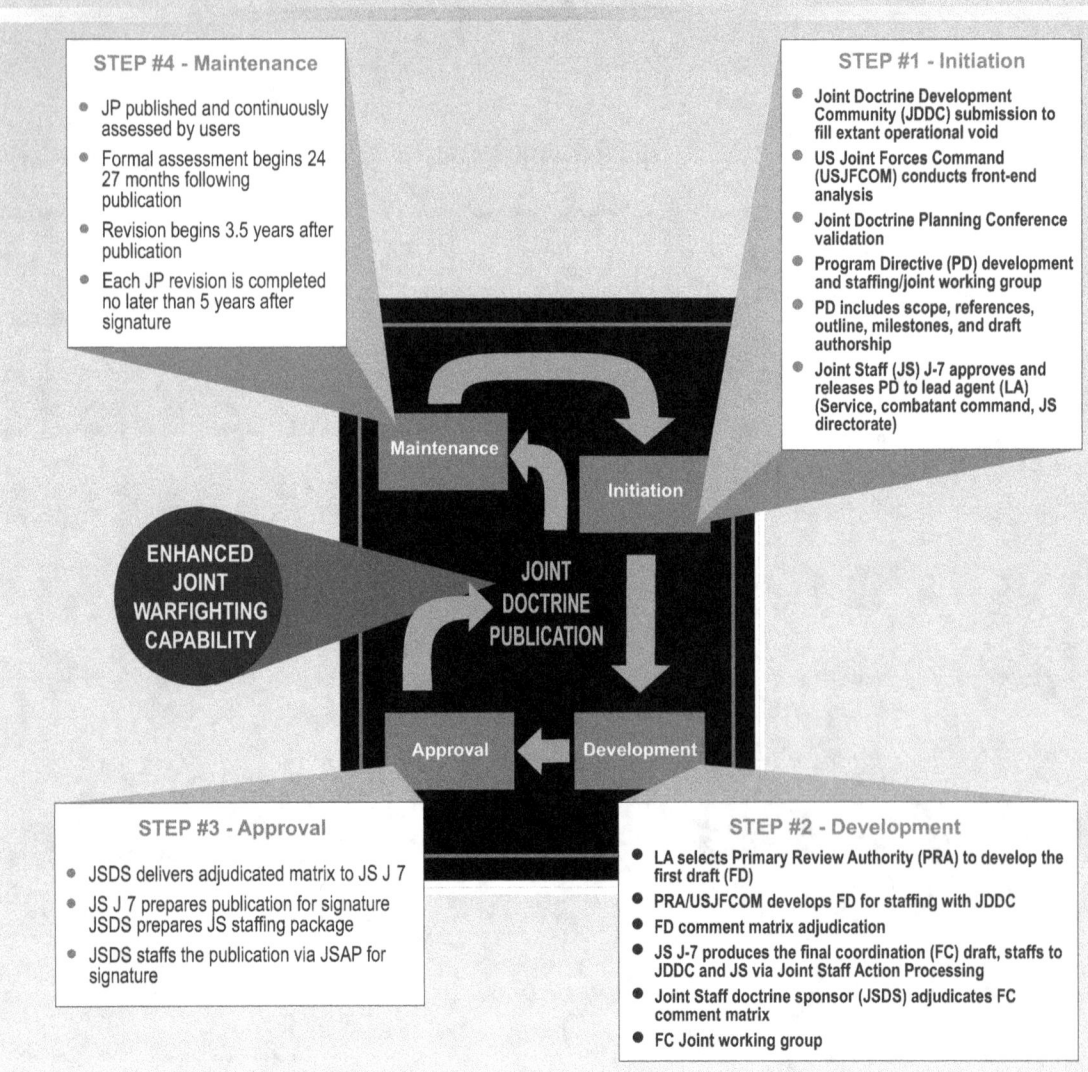

```
                        ┌──────────────┐
                        │     JP 1     │
                        │    JOINT     │
                        │   DOCTRINE   │
                        └──────────────┘
```

JP 1-0	JP 2-0	JP 3-0	JP 4-0	JP 5-0	JP 6-0
PERSONNEL	INTELLIGENCE	OPERATIONS	LOGISTICS	PLANS	COMMUNICATIONS SYSTEM

All joint publications are organized into a comprehensive hierarchy as shown in the chart above. **Joint Publication (JP) 6-0** is in the **Communications System** series of joint doctrine publications. The diagram below illustrates an overview of the development process:

STEP #4 - Maintenance

- JP published and continuously assessed by users
- Formal assessment begins 24 27 months following publication
- Revision begins 3.5 years after publication
- Each JP revision is completed no later than 5 years after signature

STEP #1 - Initiation

- Joint Doctrine Development Community (JDDC) submission to fill extant operational void
- US Joint Forces Command (USJFCOM) conducts front-end analysis
- Joint Doctrine Planning Conference validation
- Program Directive (PD) development and staffing/joint working group
- PD includes scope, references, outline, milestones, and draft authorship
- Joint Staff (JS) J-7 approves and releases PD to lead agent (LA) (Service, combatant command, JS directorate)

ENHANCED JOINT WARFIGHTING CAPABILITY

Maintenance

Initiation

JOINT DOCTRINE PUBLICATION

Approval

Development

STEP #3 - Approval

- JSDS delivers adjudicated matrix to JS J 7
- JS J 7 prepares publication for signature JSDS prepares JS staffing package
- JSDS staffs the publication via JSAP for signature

STEP #2 - Development

- LA selects Primary Review Authority (PRA) to develop the first draft (FD)
- PRA/USJFCOM develops FD for staffing with JDDC
- FD comment matrix adjudication
- JS J-7 produces the final coordination (FC) draft, staffs to JDDC and JS via Joint Staff Action Processing
- Joint Staff doctrine sponsor (JSDS) adjudicates FC comment matrix
- FC Joint working group